Love to Doug & Pam
from Maida. 1988
Chris

D0467567

PROMISES
TO KEEP

Books by Charles Paul Conn

BIOGRAPHY:

The New Johnny Cash
No Easy Game (with Terry Bradshaw)
Kathy (with Barbara Miller)
Julian Carroll of Kentucky
Hooked On a Good Thing (with Sammy Hall)
Just Off Chicken Street (with Floyd McClung)
Battle for Africa (with Brother Andrew)
The Power of Positive Students
    (with H. William Mitchell)

INSPIRATIONAL:

Making It Happen
Believe! (with Richard M. DeVos)
The Magnificent Three (with Nicky Cruz)
FatherCare

BUSINESS:

The Possible Dream
The Winner's Circle
An Uncommon Freedom
Promises to Keep

PROMISES
TO KEEP

*THE AMWAY PHENOMENON
AND HOW IT WORKS*

CHARLES PAUL CONN

G. P. PUTNAM'S SONS
New York

G. P. Putnam's Sons
Publishers Since 1838
200 Madison Avenue
New York, NY 10016

Library of Congress Cataloging in Publication Data

Conn, Charles Paul.
Promises to keep.

1. Amway Corporation. I. Title.
HF5439.H82C663 1985   381´.13´0973   85-548
ISBN 0-399-13059-4

Printed in the United States of America
1   2   3   4   5   6   7   8   9   10

dedicated to
RICHARD BALTZELL
No young writer ever had a better editor,
No one ever had a better friend.

CONTENTS

· 1 ·
CONFESSIONS OF AN AMWAY-WATCHER

An appropriate subtitle for this book might be "What Is This Thing Called Amway and Why Are All These People Saying So Many Wonderful and Terrible Things About It?" But that would not fit very well on a dust jacket. Also, some people might think the tone a bit cavalier for a subject about which so many people have such strong feelings. So I am content with the more sedate version: "The Amway Phenomenon and How It Works." In any case, you have probably picked up this book because you have in some way been engaged by one of the most fascinating stories in contemporary American life—the "experience" called Amway, which, though officially nothing more than a business, has become one of the most widely discussed and hotly debated topics of the 1980s.

Everyone, it seems, has heard of Amway. In a few years it has evolved from an obscure soap company begun in a basement to its current status as one of the can't-miss conversation starters all over America—not to mention Japan and Germany and Australia and all the rest. The unexpected rush of Amway from the basement to center stage has been one of those only-in-America things that could not have been planned or even anticipated by any of the principal characters.

If the Amway story were a tale only of corporate success and the piling up of many dollars, it would fit comfortably among many other such stories in American business history. Other men than Jay Van Andel and Richard DeVos have made fortunes from modest beginnings. Brand names other than Amway have jumped from an entrepreneur's brain into the national vocabulary in just as short a time. American life has no shortage of business success stories, but Amway is a bigger story than any of them.

Amway is a big story because it touches people in a way that Walmart Stores and Domino's Pizza and Apple Computers do not. Those are great business stories, but the cast of characters is so small. A few people, a few dozen maybe, a few hundred at the outside. Even McDonald's, with all those golden arches and television jingles and forty billion Big Macs has not touched people's lives the way Amway has.

When you talk Amway, you're talking millions of people. You're talking about a story of American life that plays on the wide screen. This is a story about which people care so deeply that they stand in big convention halls by the thousands and sing and hold hands and sometimes cry. This is a story that goes on a national television talk show and leaves the audience literally yelling for the microphone, so eager they are to tell their side of it. And when a radio host on any of those call-in stations hits a slow afternoon and wishes the phones to ring, all he needs to do is introduce the subject of Amway and the switchboard almost melts down.

What is this thing called Amway, and why are all these people saying so many wonderful and terrible things about it?

Amway is many different things to different people. The critical thing in a person's view of Amway seems to be the particular piece of Amway that person has brushed up against. Remember the old fable of the Four Blind Men of Hindustan? They each had personal, hands-on contact with an elephant, and each attempted to describe the elephant to the others. One had felt the elephant's tail, another the leg, another the trunk, and another the side. So they argued bitterly about the nature of this thing called "elephant," each with the dogmatic stubbornness of a man who knows he is right.

When people talk about Amway, nothing is more important than to know which piece of Amway that person has experienced. What one believes about it is a result of what parts of it he has seen. It is common to meet people who have fixed opinions about Amway which are entirely a product of a single circumstance, perhaps many years earlier, in which some tiny fragment of the Amway phenomenon crossed their paths. When they speak of Amway, they describe a land others have never visited; it is all strange and unrecognizable; it may not be the same Amway others have known at all.

Amway people understand that better than anyone. They know how important it is *which* Amway one has seen, how easy it is to reach an early, faulty conclusion about this thing called Amway based on a fragment here, a passing image there. The men and women in the advertising agencies, the ones who write the ads for Amway, they understand very well how that works, and they worry about it. They are paid to worry about such things. So they have developed a slogan; we hear it on radio and television and see it in *Newsweek* and *Ebony* and *Saturday Evening Post*. "TODAY'S AMWAY— GET THE *WHOLE* STORY," it tells us. The whole story. Not the fragment. Not the quickie News-at-Six television report that gives you the capsule version. Not the cocktail-party chatter about this lady's son who had a friend whose barber heard about a guy in Amway. The whole story.

Those advertising guys who came up with that slogan understood the problem. They knew that when it comes to Amway, perspective is all. The easiest thing in the world is to hang on to that elephant's tail and swear it's a snake. That problem of one's individual perspective is about the only thing that can account for a topic like Amway having so many intelligent people saying so many conflicting things about it with such obvious sincerity.

In this book I am going to tell you about Amway, and it is only fair that you should understand what my own perspective is.

I am not an Amway distributor. I have never been one. I am not an Amway employee. I am a writer, and I make my living finding interesting things to write about and writing about them. That may sound like an easy way to make a living, but I can assure you that it is not. The problem I have is that I often disagree with the public about what is and is not interesting. There are many things with which the general public is absolutely entranced, which I find about as interesting as a slowly dripping faucet. Like Boy George, for example, or those ugly little Cabbage Patch dolls. And then there have been many things which I found fascinating, and have written about, sometimes at great length, only to have the general public respond with a great collective yawn.

But on the subject of Amway, the fickle masses and I agree: this is one of those things worth talking about.

Not being an Amway person myself, there are certain limits to my information on the subject, but not many. I have been for the past several years something of a professional Amway-watcher, and there are not many pieces of the Amway story I have not brushed up against. I have pulled the elephant's trunk and leaned against his side and yanked his tail and shinnied up his leg and even sat on his back a time or two. I think I know the nature of the beast.

Somerset Maugham had a character in *The Razor's Edge* who talked about the advantage a writer has in a story like this one. "For one thing, as any writer will tell you," he said, "people do tell a writer things they would never tell anyone else." And of course he was right. I have talked to hundreds of people, inside and outside of Amway, the winners and the losers and the in-betweeners, and they have told me things they wouldn't tell anyone else. If a fellow hangs around the right places, and listens, he can learn a thing or two about

Amway that the television reporter in a big hurry never dreams of.

In all the watching and listening, I could hardly fail to develop my own point of view. After one has collected enough facts and sifted and inspected them, it is only natural that he should reach some conclusions, and I will not try to conceal mine. Every writer eventually wants to put his own spin on a story, and my spin on the Amway story is a positive one. I have poked into every corner and cranny of the "Amway world," and what I have found is, on the whole, a story of honest, admirable people who make promises and keep them.

So while I am not an Amway person, I am what might have been called in an earlier era an "Amway sympathizer." That is the perspective from which I write, not that of an insider, but rather of an outsider who likes what he has seen. I have not kissed my brains goodbye, and have not stopped watching the Amway phenomenon with a critic's eye, but I am not without an opinion on this subject either, and that is fair warning. Other Amway-watchers, who put different spins on their versions of the story, should be so honest.

■ ■ ■

So what's it all about, Amway?

Suddenly it is a word everyone uses. Amway public relations officers who a few years ago would have killed for a few seconds of network air time or to be mentioned in a national magazine woke up one morning and their brand name was a household word.

Amway jokes are trendy these days:

. . . Lena Horne tells her Broadway audience that she perspires so badly that only Amway can keep her dress clean, and the audience breaks up.

. . . Erma Bombeck says she knew she was going to have a bad day when her mother-in-law was held captive by an Amway distributor for five hours.

. . . CBS news reporter Phil Jones, reporting from the floor

of the Democratic national convention, says the management scheme of a candidate is so complicated "it rivals that
of an Amway business."

... An off-Broadway show opens in New York in late
1983, a political satire called *The Basement Tapes,* in which
the lead character is former President Gerald Ford, who runs
an Amway business from his cellar.

... Colorado senator Gary Hart, exhorting a crowd of
campaign workers to work harder, tells them: "If everyone
here will go out tonight and call ten friends and ask those ten
friends to call ten friends of theirs and ask those ten friends
to call another ten friends ... pretty soon we'll have an
Amway distributorship!"

... A best-selling novel by author Lee Smith, *Oral History,*
stars a character named Al, an ex-pro football player who
makes a killing selling Amway products.

... and even the Yippies from the Flower Power days are
getting in on it. Jerry Rubin, the former anarchist, held a
press conference at Studio 54, a Manhattan disco, to announce his ambition is to start a new gourmet diet food business "that's going to be the biggest organization in the
world. It's going to be even bigger than Amway."

That seals it. When the reformed burn-baby-burn revolu-
tionaries start dreaming about being as big as Amway, it def-
initely has become a part of the pop culture of the day.
People like Jerry Rubin always stay right on top of the
trends.

This kind of popular attention does not come merely from
having high sales volume. Many companies in the *Fortune*
500 churn more money through the corporate machinery
than does Amway, and their names are barely recognizable
to people outside their own payrolls. After all, you don't hear
Hewlett-Packard jokes on the Johnny Carson show, or see
Tank McNamara cartoons poking fun at Sperry Rand.

Amway is news because Amway is people. It is the people
of Amway, and the way those people are recruited and motivated and changed by Amway, that have made this formerly

obscure company a part of the national consciousness. Amway is not products or systems so much as it is the collective experience of a million people, some of whom are in your community or your office or maybe even your family.

When you want to understand Amway, you begin by looking at the people; and the people with whom you start are Rich DeVos and Jay Van Andel.

· 2 ·
PARTNERS

To a degree rarely found in this day of faceless conglomerates and fruitbasket-turn-over corporate leadership, Amway is the embodiment of two individuals, Jay Van Andel and Rich DeVos.

They started Amway. They own Amway. They still call the shots at Amway on a day-to-day basis. But their importance to the Amway "experience" exceeds even those roles; in a sense, the two men are living, breathing symbols of all the dreams and promises which Amway represents to a million people. They are the keepers of the flame. To a few thousand employees of Amway Corporation, DeVos and Van Andel are simply chief executive officers; but to distributors in countries around the world, they are folk heroes in the largest and best sense of the phrase.

DeVos and Van Andel are partners. Their relationship began when both were high school students in Grand Rapids, Michigan, in 1940, and almost half a century later they still work in adjoining offices, live in homes which are close enough to make them next-door neighbors, and share every decision and asset of what has become a major multinational business.

Their relationship virtually defines the word "partners." The co-equal status of each to the other is so completely accepted by the two men that the problem that one of them might gain, or seem to gain, the upper hand in their relationship simply does not occur. It is as if they have been at this so long, this partnership, that an automatic balancing mechanism operates between them; the problem of too much power or attention shifting to one or another of the partners, a common hazard of joint leadership, seems never to surface.

With Van Andel and DeVos, life is always fifty-fifty. The equation seems etched into their spirits, like some internal homeostatic mechanism: they have been at it so long they don't even have to work at it anymore. At Amway, Van Andel is Chairman of the Board, and DeVos is President. If there is any functional way in which those roles are different, it is not apparent. They share the role of chief executive officer as they share 100 percent of the company's ownership. Describing their joint and total control of the corporation, an Amway employee once looked out the window at a small Amway panel truck as it rolled past. "See that truck?" he asked. "Well, it's just a little truck, and neither one of them even knows it exists, but Rich owns half of that truck and Jay owns the other half. We try never to forget that around here."

■   ■   ■

Reader's Digest calls them "Amway's Dutch Twins." Van Andel and DeVos are products of similar backgrounds; each grew up in the homes of Dutch immigrants in the western Michigan town of Grand Rapids. The Dutch influence in that area is deep and pervasive; the nearby town of Holland has built a tourist trade on its Dutch tradition, and sections of the Grand Rapids telephone directory read like pages from the Amsterdam version. "Van" and "vander" abound.

The Dutch background is not incidental to an understanding of DeVos and Van Andel and their unusual partnership. Both men have strong emotional ties to the western Michigan region and to the values which are espoused in their ancestral traditions. Each embraces his ethnicity with an enthusiasm that is typical of the uniquely American personality at its best: fully American, but still happily and proudly Dutch-American.

The Dutch influence is there, and it is sturdy stuff, and can be credited for much of the style and values that have characterized the personality of Amway itself as it has evolved over the years. At the core of it all is the high value placed on hard work. Other traits are layered around that core: thrift, love of country, honesty in one's dealings with others, personal loyalty, faith in God and a no-nonsense approach to religion—and at the top of the list, an attitude that a man's word is his bond, that one's promises are to be kept.

Those are the essential qualities in the personal styles of DeVos and Van Andel, as in the personality of Amway itself; and while it is true that these traits are not uniquely Dutch, they are certainly *characteristically* Dutch. The firm bonding between the two partners and their cultural milieu undoubtedly created the shape of their own relationship and the early shape of Amway as well. The gift of their culture to them was a set of values and traits which, in combination, created the basis for one of the great stories in American business history.

In 1940, as the story goes, Van Andel had a car and DeVos didn't. They were teenagers attending Christian High School (a private school in Grand Rapids), and both lived at some distance from the school. Van Andel was two years older than DeVos and owned a Model A Ford. DeVos offered to pay twenty-five cents a week toward gas money in exchange for a regular ride to school. The deal was made and both a friendship and a business arrangement began. They were sixteen and fourteen years old.

Each of the partners in this share-the-ride venture was eager to join the war effort, and enlisted in the Army Air Corps while still teenagers. Military service took them separate ways. Van Andel applied for officers' school, was accepted, and found himself at Yale University for a year of training as an air corps cadet in armament and chemical warfare.

"That year changed my whole view of life," Van Andel recalls. "I discovered that by gritting my teeth I could do anything. I realized that year that I could stay up with the best of them, that it was possible to do things I never thought I could do before." He remembers many occasions when he sat in the shower rooms—the only place to go after lights-out—to study through the night.

Meanwhile, DeVos was finishing high school, and beginning to discover his own gifts as a leader. He made his first public speech as president of his senior class, and participated in occasional school debates, foreshadowing his emergence in later years as a dynamic and persuasive platform speaker. He went directly from high school into a military uniform, and was assigned to the Pacific island of Tinian, a B-29 base which was a staging area for the invasion of Japan. Then came Hiroshima and the end of the war, making the invasion unnecessary, and soon afterward the United States was welcoming home millions of discharged servicemen, among them DeVos and Van Andel.

The two friends had stayed in occasional contact during the war, and were reunited as students on the campus of hometown Calvin College. Neither had much patience with the slow rhythms and trivial pursuits of campus life, and decided during one Christmas vacation to leave college and go into business. Together.

Much has been written about their early business experiences. In the beginning they apparently had little focus on what *kind* of business they wanted to operate, but were always certain about a few things: they wanted to work for themselves, they wanted to build something from the ground up, and they wanted to do it together. Those seem to have been the irreducible elements of their early career goals as businessmen.

They began with a flying school and air-charter service

called Wolverine Air Service. It operated along the banks of the Grand River, where takeoffs and landings were sometimes practiced with use of pontoons on small planes. Later they entered what was the late-forties version of the fast-food industry, setting up a hamburger stand in a prefab building near the Grand Rapids airport, with curb service and a one-man kitchen. Soon they added a boat-rental service and sold fuel and supplies to recreational boaters on the river. They maintained all these businesses more or less simultaneously, and it added up to a fairly substantial enterprise for two young bachelors just home from the war.

In 1948 they sold the whole operation, bought a sailboat, and took an extended vacation to the Caribbean. The boat was the *Elizabeth,* a thirty-eight-foot schooner which they bought in Connecticut. Operating mostly by trial-and-error, they set sail down the east coast of the United States, beginning in December of 1948. They eventually made it to Havana, then headed for Haiti, and somewhere en route they and the *Elizabeth* parted company. One dark night, ten miles off the northern coast of Cuba, the old boat began to leak, and before the night was over it sank in fifteen hundred feet of water. Van Andel and DeVos were rescued by an American freighter, safely deposited in Puerto Rico a few days later, and continued their travels, through the Caribbean, Central and South America, and eventually home to Michigan.

So much for Tom Sawyer and Huckleberry Finn. The two friends had indulged their youthful wanderlust, and were ready to settle down to a major business challenge.

The industry to which they turned in that autumn of 1949 was the direct-sales business, which though not nearly as well known then as today, proved to be perfectly suited to their symbiotic style as partners. They became distributors of Nutrilite Products, a line of food supplements which were made and marketed by a California-based company of the same name.

The marketing system by which Nutrilite operated called for its distributors to do two things: sell the products and expand the sales force by recruiting other distributors. From the beginning, DeVos and Van Andel worked as partners in a single distributorship; there was never any thought given to doing it any other way. They were a brilliant team. They found the direct-sales industry to be one in which an appetite for hard work is rewarded directly; there were no built-in limits on how fast they could grow or how large their distributorship could become. They were in the kind of business in which they fully utilized their enormous energy and youthful ability to dream of bigger things. Within the next ten years they built a solid, prosperous business and had become mature and experienced leaders. Both were married during that period—Van Andel in 1952, DeVos in 1953—and their bachelor days gave way to family life in homes they built near one another in the little town of Ada, just outside Grand Rapids.

While Van Andel and DeVos were doing very well through the 1950s, however, the condition of Nutrilite Products as a corporation was deteriorating. A long period of internal warfare in the home office in California left the company weakened and in considerable disarray. Distributors like DeVos and Van Andel were concerned about the lack of strong corporate leadership, and tried to intervene to help solve the problems, but nothing worked. It became more and more difficult for Nutrilite distributors to operate effectively, and the growth of their businesses slowed.

The two partners finally decided that Nutrilite's corporate problems were such that it could no longer be depended on to provide leadership. Their primary obligation, they felt, was to that group of distributors whom they had brought into their business. They had a commitment to these people, many of whom had left their jobs to build full-time businesses under DeVos and Van Andel's leadership. They had recruited these people, taught them the direct-sales business, and sold them on a vision of a free and prosperous future. Those promises were not to be taken lightly; they had very little choice.

So in early 1959 the two partners made a bold, carefully

calculated gamble. They sat in the basement office of Van Andel's home and officially organized a new company. They cut the tie with Nutrilite, began plans to develop their own product line, and personally pledged to their distributors that they would build and direct a new enterprise in which their businesses would always be secure.

They called the new company Amway. From the beginning of that new company, Van Andel and DeVos were motivated by more than just the bottom line. They were determined to make Amway work for all those people who trusted and believed in them.

They had promises to keep.

.3.
PROMISES

That was over twenty-five years ago, and saying that the gamble in the basement was a good one would merely state the obvious.

Amway Corporation is today operating in forty countries and territories worldwide, still based in the town of Ada, with a billion dollars' worth of products manufactured each year and shipped around the globe from a massive four-hundred-acre plant which is almost literally within sight of that original basement where it all began.

Amway is big-time now. The corporate nerve center, called the Center of Free Enterprise, has so many visitors that it conducts regular tours several times a day. Thousands of employees work with state-of-the-art equipment in research labs, computer centers, printing plants, production lines, and shipping and transportation facilities. There is a staff of attorneys; there are platoons of accountants and clerical workers; there is an aviation department to fly and maintain the fleet of corporate airplanes; there is in place all the support staff that keeps the wheels of a well-oiled company turning.

Amway is big-time now. There are hundreds of products

and a shopper's catalog with a few thousand more. Films and video cassettes and brightly colored magazines pour out to the distributor force in a steady flood. They have a world-class hotel in Grand Rapids, and their own private island in the Caribbean, and a coast-to-coast radio network just in case it might come in handy sometime.

Amway is big-time now. Famous people come and go. Bob Hope does the television commercials, and Alexander Haig drops in to consult on international matters. The Queen of the Netherlands visits Ada now, and Mstislav Rostropovich comes by to play the cello. The National Symphony Orchestra presents a special concert for Amway leaders at the Kennedy Center, and the Beach Boys do a gig on the lawn of the Washington Monument, wearing Amway hats that say "Shop without going shopping."

Amway has come a long way from the basement.

It has been said that the more things change, the more they stay the same, and certainly that is true of Amway. Beneath the skin of its size and sophistication, just below all that slick corporate surface, the Amway of 1985 still hums away with all the old human resonances that gave it birth. The energy that fuels Amway's achievements, and sustains all its trappings of modern corporate success, is the simple trust that operates between ordinary men and women. Amway is still based on promises made and kept. It is still a business which works because its people are willing to make commitments to one another and live by them. All that corporate superstructure is only the plumage of this exotic and colorful bird; the body itself is made up of a million distributors who interact with each other and with millions of customers in a constant exchange of mutual trust.

Those sound like grand sentiments, especially to describe a business arrangement. But an exchange of trust is the glue that has always held the Amway phenonenon together, and to overlook it is to miss the point of Amway's growth and durability—and the unusual amount of influence it has in the lives of its people. It sounds corny, sure, and perhaps for that reason so many analysts miss it. Some things cannot be charted on a graph with colored pencils, but they are real nonetheless. Trust is one of those things.

One might argue that the need for trust is present in all businesses. Well, yes. But consider how centrally it operates in the Amway system. Every time a new distributor enters the Amway ranks, he or she is responding to a set of implicit promises made by another distributor. There is no salary offered, no contract signed, no guarantees made. Amway distributors have nothing to offer but their personal credibility and that of Amway Corporation, and armed only with that they say, in effect, "Join me in this thing and I will show you how it works. I'll hold your hand and work with you and if you want it badly enough we can change the financial shape of your whole life."

The "dream" that Amway distributors talk about is usually an ambitious dream. They set out in pursuit of goals that have previously eluded them, big goals like financial independence and personal freedom. When they decide to try Amway, they are responding to the promise that the old-fashioned American dream is not dead, that enough hard work in the right enterprise will yield big rewards, and that the right enterprise is Amway.

It is that promise with which Van Andel and DeVos began, and the challenge for them is maintaining the kind of company in which such promises will continue to be kept to everyone who accepts them. And the process does not end with DeVos and Van Andel: each individual Amway distributor has the same set of promises to keep, to every new person he or she has brought aboard.

This highly personalized approach to business can be either a blessing or a curse. A system like Amway's brings into play a volatile mix of human emotions. People's dreams and hopes are on the line. With such a high-octane fuel at work in the system, the energy that can be released is potentially enormous; but if the formula is wrong, if the promises are not kept, the history of a company can be very short and very explosive.

Amway has a twenty-five-year history that indicates the

mix is right. The system works. The promises are being kept.

In his novel *Mortal Friends,* author James Carroll describes the source of a particular character's success. He succeeded, Carroll says, because he taught others that "the most value-laden human act is the simple, faithful act of commitment to one person."

If one seeks the key to the success of the Van Andel–DeVos partnership, it will not be found primarily in their speaking skills or IQ scores or managerial expertise. Those things are important, but they are secondary. The key to the Amway story is less tangible than those things; it is less a matter of their technical skill than a matter of their mind-set. They have understood, first with each other, about that "simple, faithful act of commitment to one person" and they have taught it to others and built a company around it.

.4.

CHOOSING TO CHANGE

Jay Van Andel and Rich DeVos are only two of the characters in the Amway drama.

There are others—tens of thousands of others—who are part of the story, not just by having joined as distributors at one time or another, but by making their Amway connection a major part of their lives.

How many people have been Amway distributors? That number is impossible to determine, but it must add up to several million. There are presently approximately one million Amway distributors worldwide. Three quarters of those are in the United States. Amway has a fairly stable annual retention rate of 50 percent, which means that half those distributors who join in any given year renew their membership at the end of that year.

Considering Amway's twenty-five-year history, it would seem a conservative estimate that at least three million North Americans are now or have been in Amway. (The corporation does not publish such a figure, and estimating it is difficult for two reasons: one, the recruiting rates have been different each year; two, there is no way to know how many people have been in and out more than once. It is not uncommon for a person to rejoin after having quit.)

The number of people directly affected by Amway is further enlarged when one considers that these numbers refer not to distributors, but to distributor*ships*. Amway reports that about 75 percent of its distributorships are husband-wife teams, and in most cases both spouses are personally involved in the operation of the business. Add to that the number of children at home whose parents are a distributorship, and the total number of "Amway people" expands again.

If there are a million distributors worldwide at any given time, there may be as many as two or three million people living in Amway-distributor households in North America. In a combined Canada-America population of about two hundred and fifty million, that is a fairly substantial percentage, with a potential for major impact on these two nations.

But lest we get carried away with this numbers game, there are some offsetting factors to consider. First, the million-distributor figure includes every Jack or Jill who signs on the dotted line, pays seventy-five dollars or so for a sales kit, and is assigned a distributor number. He or she may do this late one night in a friend's living room, decide before getting home that same night that it was all a mistake, and never sell a product or recruit another distributor. That person is nonetheless a distributor as far as the Amway computer is concerned, at least until the end of the year, when the name will be scrubbed from the list.

There are other distributors who come into the business, try it for a few weeks or months, don't like it, and, for all practical purposes, quit. But sometimes these people, feeling that they were into a good thing if they had only pursued it, continue to renew their distributorships year after year, always intending to get involved again in an active way, but for various reasons never doing so. These people get counted in the computer as renewing distributors.

Then there are those people who become distributors because they like the products and want to buy them at wholesale prices. They may even sell a few products at retail to a few of their friends. But they never go to an Amway meeting, never try to persuade anyone else to join the business, and may know or care very little about the company except that it has good products which they enjoy buying at wholesale prices. These people are Amway distributors, too, of course, though not a part of the "Amway phenomenon" in any meaningful sense.

The type of Amway person who brings the company to the level of public attention it enjoys in 1985 is the distributor who, unlike the ones just described, sees in the business an opportunity to make significant changes in some aspect of his or her life. Those changes usually have to do with money. Amway is a business, and people get into it to make money.

When people say they became Amway distributors for more freedom, they are usually talking about the kind of freedom that money brings. The British author Walpole said it was natural for free men to think about money, because money *is* freedom. There are hundreds of everyday, practical freedoms that money can buy.

In the same way, those people who explain that they came into Amway in an attempt to get control over their own lives are also referring to the control that money brings. And those who say that they became distributors to create a better family life are, at bottom, talking about money as well. Money to keep the wife from having to go to work. Money to make it possible to survive without moonlighting. Money to leave a job or profession that demands sixty hours a week.

If it is true that people who plunge into the "Amway experience" do so to produce some sort of change in their lives, it is usually to make the money that causes change to occur. They come into Amway not to chase the dollar, but to pursue some dream of a better life, which the dollar will open to them.

It is fashionable in some circles to portray Amway distributors as greedy and obsessed with money. But honest Amway-watchers who have studied the business agree that "greedy" does not accurately describe most Amway distributors. To the contrary, the themes which are sounded most frequently and with most conviction are those of more family life, more control over one's own future, and more opportunity for personal expression. It takes money to secure these things, so earning that money becomes the immediate focus.

"The future of any great idea is always made more bright when it's found to be profitable," sociologist Joel Garreau once quipped. Perhaps that is one of the reasons for Amway's success. It espouses the great ideas of personal freedom, working for oneself, and helping others achieve their goals—and proposes a highly profitable way of acting out those ideas.

How many Amway distributors make enough money to produce the changes in their lives which they seek?

That's impossible to say, of course; it's like asking "when is a person happy?" Well, obviously, when he has whatever it takes to make him happy. Different people have different thresholds, and whatever takes them over that threshold has worked for them, constitutes success for them, whether it is a little or a lot.

Abraham Lincoln is said to have been amused by the comment that his legs were too long. "How long should a man's legs be?" he asked. "Long enough to reach the ground! And that's exactly how long mine are." How much money must one make in Amway to be regarded a success? As much as it takes to meet the goals that brought him or her into the business in the first place.

By that standard, one suspects that there are many thousands of successful Amway distributors who never make big pots of money or drive a new Jaguar. To the mother who joins to pay her child's tuition at a private school, three hundred dollars a month extra income makes for a very successful Amway business. For the young architect who hates architecture and wants to leave it, success in Amway might require an annual income of fifty thousand dollars a year. Amway promises to both of them an honest shot at changing their lives in terms of their own goals. If the mother gets the tuition money and the architect gets the new career, both promises are kept. Both can be described, with equal accuracy, as successful Amway distributors.

That being said, the question of how many Amway distributors make sizable incomes remains an interesting one. The level of Amway success which many people regard as a benchmark of achievement comes when a distributor earns the title of Direct Distributor. At this level one's gross Amway income is usually comfortably over one thousand dollars a month, and is often much more than that. There are currently over twenty thousand such distributorships in Amway.

The money goes up from there. Those tales you may have heard about your ol' buddy Joe from college days who left his job in the pharmacy and got rich in Amway may not be as wildly exaggerated as you had hoped. At the higher levels of the Amway scale, there is a legitimate opportunity to make big money on a continuing basis.

Can people actually earn six-figure incomes, year after year, from their Amway business alone? Yes, they can, although the corporation will not say how many do so. There has been one recent published report, which the company has not denied, putting the number of distributorships currently earning over one hundred thousand dollars per year at about three hundred. And the report points out that when it says "over," that sometimes means "way over."

Amway Corporation is reluctant to talk about specific income figures for distributors. Amway officials realize that companies such as theirs, which compete with other direct-sales companies for new distributors, are often suspected of inflating their numbers when they talk about potential income. Apparently to avoid that perception, Amway Corporation tends to downplay the size of its top distributors' incomes. It is an irony that in an industry often suspected of fudging its figures upwards, Amway seems more likely to *under*state than to overstate how much its people earn.

If there is any part of the Amway promise which is even

more appealing than the money, it is the potential for making that money without being tied to a ten-hour-a-day, six-day-a-week grind. An Amway distributorship, though it requires long hours and hard work, still gives a man or woman the opportunity to choose those hours and pace that work according to their own desires.

In any kind of free-lance work, there is a certain amount of personal freedom—not less work, necessarily, but work according to one's own schedule. The task of building and maintaining an Amway business is essentially of that nature; it offers the wage earner or salaried employee the possibility of finding an alternative to the nine-to-five routine.

Owners of retail stores and certain types of professionals, though they have the potential for large incomes, often pay such a high price in job pressure and long hours that they grow disenchanted with those occupations. The physician or dentist who makes a six-figure income but never has time to enjoy it might justifiably wonder whether the pay is worth the price. There is an old proverb that says you can always get free cheese in a mousetrap—it could well be a comment on the price some pay for success.

Little wonder, then, that Amway offers a very attractive alternative to all those hardworking little mousies who, having reached the big chunk of cheese, find they are not free to enjoy it. That promise of big income combined with a less demanding and restrictive schedule is perhaps the biggest single reason for the influx of professional people into the Amway distributor force in the past few years.

To whom does Amway make its promises? To all those who want changes in their lives—whether big changes or only very small ones—and are willing to work for them. Amway promises to provide the opportunity; the distributor promises to provide the work.

Many people have come and gone through the doors of Amway without much success. But the record is clear on this: that when the distributor does his or her part of the bargain, the Amway promise is kept.

.5.
FACES

Amway is people, and the people come in different sizes, shapes, and packaging.

An Amway-watcher learns early about the diversity of Amway people, and is usually surprised by it. There is no misconception about Amway which is so wide of the mark as the notion that its people are all alike, that they are just so many cookie-cutter versions of the same basic model. The first Amway meeting I attended was in Minneapolis, and I was surprised that the people in the crowd didn't look the way I expected. "But these people don't look like the Amway *type!*" I protested to a friend sitting beside me.

He looked at me with the patient condescension usually reserved by mothers for their children. "And what did you think *was* the Amway type?" he asked. I had no ready answer. "Well, you know . . . ," I started, and that's about as far as I could go. I had expected all these Amway people to look like little clones of DeVos and Van Andel, and that had been a foolish stereotype.

Since then I have seen many of the faces of Amway, and nothing I have learned is so certain than this—that there is no single cloth or pattern from which Amway people are cut.

"We don't choose these people," Van Andel once said. "They choose themselves. In Amway everyone is a volunteer. And when people volunteer, you get all different kinds of people. That's the way we want it to be."

GEOGRAPHICALLY, there are Amway distributors in each of the fifty states, all the Canadian provinces, and some forty other countries and territories. Amway is sometimes described as primarily a Midwestern and Deep South phenomenon, perhaps because of its origins in the Midwest and its middle-American flavor. But California is the single state with the largest amount of Amway activity, and some of the most rapid recent growth has occurred in the Pacific Northwest and in the urban cities along the Eastern Seaboard.

The idea that Amway works best in the middle-American heartland does not fit the facts anymore, though it began there. This is true in Canada as well. Though most of the earliest growth of the Canadian business naturally occurred in the central provinces of Manitoba and Ontario, it quickly spread to both coasts. Amway is probably healthier today in the sharply contrasting cultures of British Columbia in the west and Quebec in the east than anywhere else in Canada—an indication of the ability of the business to thrive in a variety of sociopolitical climates.

The RURAL-URBAN balance in the distributor force shows a similar mix. Often regarded as happening only in small towns and suburbs, distributorships can also be built in the big cities or in rural areas. I met a distributor couple once who told me they lived in New York City. I asked where, exactly, expecting to hear an address in one of the outlying boroughs. Eighty-sixth and Central Park West, in Manhattan, I was told. More urban than that one cannot get. Since then I have learned that Amway businesses in the city are not as rare as I had supposed.

Nor is it rare, on the other end of that continuum, to find bustling distributorships in tiny rural outposts. I once drove north from Wichita, Kansas, across flat and what seemed to me rather desolate farm country, for two hours, to meet an

Amway leader named Vince Berland. He had built a big, fast-growing distributorship out there in central Kansas, I had been told, but I could hardly imagine that many *people* out there, much less that many Amway distributors. When I reached the meeting place, Berland appeared, and out in the middle of all that farmland, there had somehow also materialized hundreds and hundreds of enthusiastic Amway distributors. I saw more human beings in that one meeting hall than I had seen for the last hundred miles put together.

The RACIAL AND ETHNIC diversity in the Amway distributor force is increasing. As the business moved out from its birthplace in the upper Midwest, it became increasingly an ethnic mosaic that resembles the general population. Large numbers of Asian-Americans have been successful in the business in recent years, particularly on the West Coast and in Hawaii. In Canada, French-speaking Quebecers comprise one of the most veteran and active groups in the entire world of Amway.

One aspect of minority-group involvement in the Amway business is the high degree of assimilation of such distributors into the larger Amway body. With a few exceptions, there are no all-black or all-Hispanic Amway organizations as such. Generally, distributors of various backgrounds work together in the same groups. There is no single distributorship in the United States which might be described as an Hispanic group, for example, yet the total number of Spanish-speaking distributors is so large that Amway routinely translates and produces all its materials in that language.

Though the public sometimes associates RELIGION with Amway, it is difficult to describe the distributor force as being predominantly of a particular faith. It might be said that Amway people on the whole tend to take their religious faith somewhat more seriously than does the general population, but that faith is not likely to be of any particular brand name. Conservative Protestants seem to get most of the attention, perhaps because their tradition encourages them to be more open in expressing their religious attitudes. But

Catholics are also represented in large numbers, as are Mormons, especially in the West, and virtually every other form of Christianity, and other religions including Buddhism and Islam.

The percentage of Jewish distributors has risen rapidly in recent years, a trend which is perhaps related to the growth of the business in areas of the East where the Jewish population is greater. Pete and Barb Matz are leaders of a New Jersey-based Amway organization, which is one of the best examples of the dramatic growth of the business on the east coast in the 1980s. The Matz group is a true ethnic and religious melting pot, with a particularly large percentage of Jewish members.

Are non-Christian distributors bothered by Amway's "Christian" image? Not at all, says Matz. "We make it clear that religion is *not* what Amway is about. One's religious faith is a personal matter, and everyone in our group respects that. Lots of our people are Jewish; lots are Christian. In many cases, we don't even know which is which—it's just not an issue. We believe this business is for everybody, and the label you wear shouldn't make any difference."

In the matter of AGE, the Amway distributor force is similarly diverse. The company's rules do not allow minors (below age eighteen) to recruit other distributors, which effectively sets a limit on the lower end. But at the top there is no limit whatever, and Amway, like other direct-sales companies, is a popular second-income opportunity for senior citizens. The percentage of Americans in the sixty-five-and-older category will continue to rise over the next two decades, according to census analysts, and that is a very positive trend for businesses like Amway. Already there are many examples of people who join the business in their sixties, usually to offset the reduced income they face in retirement, and build distributorships which produce far more money than their total pension packages which they have spent a lifetime developing.

Bernice Hansen of Michigan is a prototype of the senior-citizen distributor. Now in her early seventies, she looks and sounds like just another sweet li'l ol' grandmother, but beneath that gentle appearance there is something of an Amway tycoon. Widowed since 1968, she and her son-in-law and daughter, Skip and Susan Ross, maintain an enormous Amway business which is said to be one of the most profitable in the country. When she qualified for Social Security benefits, her monthly stipend seemed so small in comparison to her Amway income that she told the government to keep it. "They need it worse than I do," she explains with a grandmotherly twinkle.

Several newspaper articles about Amway in recent years have mentioned the "new breed" of Amway distributor, describing a trend toward young, professional couples who enter the business as a primary career choice rather than as a second income. That is a clear trend, and a logical one, since the task of building a distributorship is so well suited to the energy and enthusiasm of young people. Van Andel and DeVos began their own distributorship as young bachelors.

Jim and Bev Kinsler of New York are examples of this "new breed," coming as they did into Amway as a very young couple. He was just beginning a coaching career, and was good at it; he had three championship teams in his first six years. When the Kinslers came into Amway, they tended to attract other young couples like themselves, and their organization has a youthful vitality that reflects their own style. To young couples like the Kinslers, Amway was an early career choice which turned out to be a very good one. They regard their age—or lack of it—as an advantage.

Just as with age, generalizations about EDUCATION do not fit well in describing Amway distributors. Much has been made of the movement of college-educated professionals into Amway in the last ten years. But a strong distributorship remains one of those things which is genuinely within the reach of the man or woman without much formal education. It is a refreshing thing, in this world of status-oriented pigeonholes, to see people lined up across a stage at an Amway meeting, being honored for their achievement, without regard to which one has the Ph.D. and which failed to finish high school.

Coleman and Charlotte Orr represent the classic Amway story of starting with nothing. Both of them dropped out of school in the early grades and never went back. Orr has such a charismatic, rambunctious personality that it is easy to imagine him breaking up the furniture in a honky-tonk saloon in his native San Antonio, which is where he might have been, he says, if it hadn't been for Amway. Instead, he and Charlotte live in one of Atlanta's posh northside suburbs, where he directs a lucrative Amway business that sprawls all over the United States. He becomes emotional when he talks about the chance the business gave him: "Where else but in Amway does a guy like me get from where I was to here?"

So what is the Amway type, anyway?

The more Amway-watching I do, the less sure I am that any kind of profile fits at all. Even those patterns which did exist in the early years of Amway are eroding fairly rapidly, as the distributor force becomes more and more diverse. As that process occurs, it inevitably accelerates; the corporation is less and less able to target any particular demographic group, and consequently aims its appeal more and more broadly, and the process feeds on itself.

So the stereotype continues to break down. Already, 50 percent of all Amway distributors are women; 25 percent are unmarried; approximately one-third are outside the United States and Canada. There is an image of the Amway distributor as a middle-aged white man in a small Midwestern town, with a high-school education, a favorite pew in the local Baptist church, and a Reagan bumper sticker on his car, who has a wife and two kids and a job at the factory— you get the picture.

The image just won't wash anymore.

.6.
THE OTHER PARTNERSHIP

When the word "partnership" is used to describe Amway, one thinks of the personal partnership of Van Andel and DeVos.

There is another partnership at work in the Amway phenomenon which is just as much a part of the story as the teamwork of the two co-founders. That second partnership is the one between the corporation in Ada and the distributor force which spreads around the world.

These two parts of the "world of Amway" are inseparable and interdependent. Each is impressive on its own, but neither amounts to very much without the other. The corporation makes the products and provides the support base; the distributor force sells the products, recruits new people, and provides the cash flow.

It is conceivable that Amway Corporation could find other ways to market its products without its distributor force, just as it is conceivable that the distributors could find another product line to take the place of Amway. But in either case, to imagine one seeking to operate without the other is a wildly hypothetical conjecture. They are two separate structures, but too inextricably linked to one another to think of surviving apart.

The connective tissue joining Amway Corporation and the Amway distributor force is, of course, DeVos and Van Andel themselves. They fit into both sides of the equation. They own and lead the corporation, and at the same time are distributors—the original distributors, in fact. In the one role, they are chief executive officers of a manufacturing company. In the other role, they are the distributorship from which every other distributorship in Amway can be directly traced.

It is the structure which is unusual—perhaps even unique—in the direct-sales industry, and more than any other single element it may account for the soundness and resilience of Amway in good times and bad.

It is conventional wisdom in economic theory to speak of the inherent contrast between the corporate mentality and the entrepreneurial mentality. Good entrepreneurs do not necessarily make good corporate officials, and vice versa. For a company like Amway to operate well, both types of talent are needed. The problem is often that the two do not always understand each other's mind-set; the juncture between the two is often ragged and disjointed.

At Amway, Van Andel and DeVos provide the link between the corporate and entrepreneurial sides of the business. In them there is a fusion of the two "mentalities" which gives great strength to the whole operation. Of all the things they do, none is more important than this: to nurture the partnership between Amway Corporation and its distributors.

As Amway grows larger, the tendency is for the two co-founders to become increasingly removed from the distributor force. In the past year or so they expressed concern about that tendency, and are moving aggressively to keep it under control. One highly placed Amway official, noting the need for continued hands-on involvement by the two owners, acknowledges that they are consciously reorganizing their time to stay in closer contact with the distributor force:

"Let's face it," he states. "These guys have become important people in circles far above where they were ten years ago. There are no doors that are not open to them. They've become involved in the national political process in a major way; they're being wined and dined by some of the most important people in the country. You've got Jay heading up the national Chamber of Commerce; you've got Rich getting hundreds of speaking invitations every year. These guys are really heavy hitters now, and everybody would like a piece of them.

"It takes a real commitment, in the position they're in, to keep pumping all their time and energy into running this company. They've had to make a major decision to turn their attention back to Amway, and that's what they have done. Both of them. They are at the point in their lives when they've had all the honors and fame and all that stuff. Right now what they want is to take this company to the next level of size and influence. They know that if it's going to be done, they have to do it themselves, and that's what they intend to do."

They have to do it themselves. They are, as baseball star Reggie Jackson used to say, the straw that stirs the drink.

■   ■   ■

DeVos and Van Andel have pledged to make the corporate machinery which they supervise "more responsive" to the needs of the distributor force, and a fresh surge of energy and optimism in the Amway system in 1985 suggests that the team in Ada is indeed finding new ways to support the distributor force.

Part of that revitalized corporate effort is a result of an in-house evaluation and restructuring led by Bill Nicholson, a forty-one-year-old Houston business whiz who recently joined the Ada leadership team. Nicholson is one of those can-do-anything types whose résumé glows in the dark. He is a former All-American basketball player, former fighter pilot in the Vietnam War, former White House aide in the Ford administration, former millionaire corporate president. Now he operates as Mr.-Fix-It at Amway Corporation, and his grasp of the dynamics of the Van Andel–DeVos–distributor partnership is impressive.

He has seen many successful and famous men do business over the years, in the White House and elsewhere, and he calls Van Andel and DeVos "absolutely the two most capable business leaders I've ever met." Why? "They know how to take what I call the long-term view. They don't work just for today; they're not always running around putting out fires. They take the long-term view. They are in this thing not just for 1985, but for the eighties and the nineties and the twenty-first century. These two guys are able to separate the immediate needs from the long-term ones and deal with all of it at the same time.

"Every business goes through cycles, and the last couple of years have been a down cycle for the direct-sales industry and for Amway. The tendency with some leaders is to panic, start doing things to deal with the immediate problems, even though they might throw the whole system out of whack. Rich and Jay don't do that. They are absolutely committed to the long term, and they have made decisions in the last year or so that are going to make Amway the leader in this industry for many years to come. It takes a lot of poise to pass up the quick fix when things are down, and make the long-term decisions instead, and that's what they have done."

Part of the changes to which Nicholson refers is a move into new product lines, in some cases an expensive process which cuts the profit picture temporarily but ensures the ability of the company to compete in the future. In 1984, for example, Amway opened a new $12 million cosmetics plant which includes state-of-the-art technology to support a major expansion of their cosmetics business. The obvious strategy, though the company does not say so directly, is to gear up to go head-to-head with competitors such as Avon and Mary Kay, for whom cosmetics are primary. The company has also announced a major new training initiative in the cosmetics area for its distributors.

A new $5.7 million expansion of Amway's aerosol plant was also completed in 1984, designed to keep the company abreast of the field in that product area.

In addition to these developments in product lines which are basic parts of the Amway inventory, the company is expanding into more and more "big-ticket" items with considerable success. Last year it entered the security field with a Perimeter Alarm Security System which sold so fast there was a waiting list for them, topping $30 million in sales in the first year. In early 1985 Amway released a water purification system, saying it uses a technology which puts it one jump ahead of the competition in that area.

Other big-ticket products are on the way, corporate officials promise, and the expectation is that such new items will make the profit picture for the individual distributor brighter. "We're coming up with ways to put more money in the pocket of the distributor without necessarily increasing his workload," a staff member explained, "and the move to big-ticket items is one way to do that. We will always be in the soap business, but we want to give the distributor all the different ways to make money we can."

Other innovations which are just now coming onstream include a program in which the Amway distributor can sign up customers for MCI long-distance telephone services and make a commission on that. There is also a new way for customers to buy some of the more expensive Amway products on credit, through a financing plan in which the customer's purchase will be financed by Amway Corporation itself, making the sale of these items easier for the distributor.

Product development is not the only area in which the corporation is moving aggressively to support its partners in the distributor force. Public relations efforts of the company are being intensified as well. "We don't have the image we would like," DeVos acknowledged recently in a magazine interview, and he and Van Andel are personally spearheading a new initiative to build the Amway reputation as a generous, responsible corporate citizen.

Part of this effort was the leading role Amway played in the national Easter Seals telethon in the spring of 1984 and 1985. Each year, some twenty thousand distributors joined together to raise over one million dollars for the Easter Seals campaign.

Amway has become conspicuously active in patronizing the arts in the last few years. The company picked up the tab for the National Symphony Orchestra tour of major European capitals and held receptions for its leading distributors in those countries along the way, sponsored the visit of the Hong Kong Children's Choir to the United States, and commissioned a series of original paintings called "America at Work" by artist Paul Collins.

(Nor is all the music Amway sponsors high-brow, either. In 1984 the company paid for a "free" open-air concert, celebrating the Fourth of July, by the Beach Boys. How's that for eclectic taste?)

Other parts of the Amway operation bring it positive public attention. The company owns Mutual Broadcasting Network, the nation's largest radio network, with some nine hundred affiliated stations. The Amway Grand Plaza Hotel, a project which cost over sixty million dollars, is now part of the prestigious Preferred Hotels organization, and has received an AAA five-diamond rating (the best given to all but half a dozen American hotels), and has in the past year received rave reviews from everyone from the Chicago *Tribune* to *Esquire* magazine. And of course there is Peter Island, the Amway-owned yacht club and resort in the British Virgin Islands, which the Dallas *Times* recently called "just too good to be true."

But the best public relations for Amway Corporation continues to be the owners themselves. Both men represent Amway in a fashion that symphony orchestras and Rose Bowl Parade floats and national advertising cannot. Amway will always be a very human company, with a very personal style. And the symbol of its history and its promise is the two men who conceived it and who lead it.

To the various publics to which DeVos and Van Andel symbolize Amway, none is so important as the "third partner" in the Amway enterprise—the distributor force. The general public, when it sees the two founders, may see wealthy and powerful men, shakers and movers, giants of industry who dine with presidents and entertain queens.

But there is a certain sense in which an Amway distributor, when he sees Van Andel and DeVos, sees another Amway distributor. He knows that Van Andel and DeVos started just as he did, with that first customer, that first newly recruited fellow distributor, that first dollar in profit. The newest Amway distributor in 1985 knows that the President and the Chairman of the Board have been where he is, have done what he is doing, and in some way that seems to make an important difference.

The partnership between the owners of Amway and the distributor force works so well because it is a truly *synergistic* relationship. The dictionary says synergism is "the joint action of two agents in which the total effect is greater than the sum of their effects when acting independently."

That is a pretty fair description of the Amway phenomenon and how it works.

.7.

SECOND GENERATION

Virtually every observer of the direct-sales industry agrees that one of the most important advantages which Amway enjoys is the unique leadership of the Van Andel–DeVos team. It is an asset which Amway's competitors have no way to match, and most observers agree that it gives Amway an edge. As an Amway official once said, quoted in a *Reader's Digest* article: "Other corporations can duplicate our products, even our marketing plan. What they can't duplicate are the Dutch Twins."

The problem is that such an asset, should it be lost, can immediately become a liability. If either DeVos or Van Andel should be unable for some reason to continue his personal involvement in the company's management, what then? They are both healthy, relatively young, and show no signs of wishing to pass the torch; but if they did, could they?

It is a problem of which the co-founders are aware, and as a result they have sought to minimize the degree to which their own personal leadership is critical to the company's success. "We do not enjoy and will not encourage this 'cult of personality' which some feel has developed around the two of us," Van Andel has explained. "Amway has been built solidly on sound business principles, and it will continue to thrive with or without our being involved in a personal way. We have assembled an excellent team of leaders here at Amway Corporation who can get the job done."

But still the torch is difficult to pass. Whether or not they personally enjoy their importance to hundreds of thousands of Amway distributors, it is there, a deep and often emotional attachment not to just any executive who might happen to head Amway, but specifically to DeVos and Van Andel as leaders and symbols of all that Amway has come to mean.

Political historian Garry Wills once wrote about this kind of personal leadership: "When authority flows from a *person*, that authority cannot be delegated. The magic touch must be bestowed by the ruler himself. He must go out among the people, lead the action. Everything must be referred to him, decided by him, must bear his mark, embody his style."

Though the co-founders have attempted to develop a senior executive staff capable of operating the business, as Van Andel says, it has become apparent that "the magic touch" is not transferrable to them. However competent they may be, they are not DeVos and Van Andel, and in the unusual chemistry of the Amway world, that continues to be important.

The solution to this particular leadership problem lies obviously with the children of the co-founders, the second generation of DeVoses and Van Andels. There are four children in each family, and among the eight of them there would seem to reside ample brainpower, technical skill, and personal charisma to lead Amway into the twenty-first century—providing, of course, that the appropriate training and motivation is there.

It is a solution which, predictably, DeVos and Van Andel considered and provided for long ago. The older children in each family are already involved in the company's operations, and they seem to be fully committed to long careers in

Amway management. The motivation is present, and the training is under way.

■ ■ ■

The oldest children of each of the Amway co-founders have already reached the vice-presidential level in the corporate structure. Nan Van Andel, thirty-one, is vice president of communications, while Dick DeVos, twenty-nine, serves as vice president, international. The younger Van Andel children (Steve, David, and Barbara), as well as the other DeVoses (Dan, Cheri, and Doug), are also in various stages of Amway careers or training programs.

Dick DeVos and Nan Van Andel did not exactly wake up one Christmas morning to find vice presidencies under the tree. Each has worked at the company for almost ten years, including a rigorous five-year training program which took them into every major area of the company's operation. Currently, DeVos supervises Amway's activity in all its forty international markets; all chief executives involved with operations outside the United States report to him. Van Andel has responsibility for all advertising and the production of all sales literature, including magazines and newsletters for the distributor force throughout North America, and oversight of audiovisual and creative operations. Both have joined their fathers on Amway's Policy Committee, though only the co-founders vote.

Nan Van Andel first came to work full-time almost ten years ago, immediately after graduating from college. "When I got out of college," she recalls, "there was never any big decision that had to be made to go into Amway. This is my life. It always has been. I have all that early bonding with the business from childhood. I understand where it came from and all the things my Dad and Rich did to make it grow. So it just never occurred to me to consider another career. Coming to work at Amway was as natural as breathing."

Dick DeVos also remembers childhood days with a father deeply involved in Amway: "Dad took us on trips; we got to know the Amway people. He knew what he was doing, I think; he must have realized those things build in you a feeling for the business and a real affection for it. By the time I had to decide what I wanted to do with my life, I liked Amway and thought I could make a contribution. So I started out to learn the business."

Both Dick and Nan worked at entry-level positions in the Amway plant before their fathers devised a systematic training program to prepare them for their eventual leadership roles. The training program was a five-year process designed to give all the Van Andel and DeVos children a wall-to-wall experience of Amway. Under the supervision of a senior staff member, the trainees spend time in every part of the operation from the boardroom to the warehouse, even including a period spent as distributors, selling products to retail customers and attempting to sponsor new prospects into the distributor force.

The uniquely devised training program was a tough regimen that made Amway veterans of the two oldest children. Both Nan and Dick relished the challenge of it and emerged as poised, informed executives. "It is a strange thing," wrote novelist John D. MacDonald, "the way a bright young brain, exposed to a certain kind of knowledge at just the right time, bends in the direction of that knowledge, sops it up, relishes it."

Today both vice presidents work shoulder-to-shoulder with older Amway executives, and though they are obviously destined by birth and training for higher things, their prominent surnames seem not to get in the way. "I think we have all been extremely sensitive to the family connections," says Dick DeVos, "and I don't think we've had any problems. You develop a bit of a sixth sense about when people are using you or not. Dad and Jay know they have to maintain an arm's-length relationship. They stay out of the way. Both Dad and Jay do a great job of that."

Nan agrees: "I think initially people are concerned about one's last name or one's position. Then they come to know you as a person and relate to you as the person you are. People around here don't think much about the family connection. During the training program, I would come into a place to work with people, and after one or two days, I was just Nan, not the boss's daughter. Then it is what I am and do that matters."

Both Nan and Dick are married, and each has provided a third-generation addition to the respective families. Nan is married to Gary Tilken, a commodities broker whom she met on a blind date. They have a year-old daughter, Leigh Elizabeth. Dick met his wife, Betsy, when she was a Calvin College coed. Their son Ricky (Richard DeVos III) is almost three years old.

The two Amway vice presidents are close personal friends, though they rarely are together on a purely social basis. They are not as dissimilar in personal styles as are their fathers, and their shared Amway experiences as children give them a unique background for their own brand of teamwork. "In a sense," Nan explains, "the Van Andel kids and the DeVos kids grew up together. We lived down the block and we were the only two families on the block. We were the whole neighborhood, and we just grew up together."

"We've always had a close friendship," says Dick. "Around the office, of course, we are a bit more 'official,' but in private it's always been 'Uncle Jay' to us, and our dad has been 'Uncle Rich' to them. I don't think I've ever bothered to ring the doorbell at the Van Andel house; I just stick my head inside and say 'hi!' That's the kind of relationship we've always had."

Another characteristic shared by Dick and Nan is a sense of duty about Amway, a commitment to the long-term view taken by their fathers. None of the Van Andel or DeVos offspring seem to have discarded their parents' world view in the type of knee-jerk rejection that occurs so frequently in the families of the rich and powerful. The parental value system seems to have been transmitted with very little dilution to the second generation. Asked how he would describe his own sociopolitical stance compared to the conservative positions taken by his father, Dick responds, "If there is any position to the right of where he is, that's probably where I am!"

"I believe Amway is important," states Nan. "What we do is important, and we are determined to keep it moving. I don't know whether corporate competition is that important to me, in the conventional sense. I'd like Amway to be number one, and all that, but that's not what really is important to me or, I think, to Dick. What *is* important is to make sure that we are meeting the needs of our distributor force. We want everybody from the guy who signed up yesterday to the one who has been in from the beginning to get what they want out of Amway. We want Amway to measure up to their expectations. We want it to continue to be an opportunity that gives people hope. That's the kind of challenge Amway is to me."

It seems likely that Nan and Dick—and the other second generation Van Andels and DeVoses who follow—will have the skill and the commitment necessary to meet that challenge. As young executives, they already show signs of being able to maintain the "magic touch" of their famous fathers. If they do, it will be because they have been thoroughly prepared for Amway's particular demands.

"Remember," said Paul Theroux in *The Mosquito Coast*, "experience isn't an accident. It's a reward that's given to people who pursue it. That's a deliberate act, and it's hard work." Dick DeVos and Nan Van Andel would no doubt agree.

.8.

THE YANKS ARE COMING

When Amway made its first step into the foreign market-place in 1970, it was regarded as an experiment, a leap in the dark. Certainly no one anticipated that within fifteen years, international sales would account for nearly one third of Amway's volume and would be the fastest growing sector in the company.

That first cautious move was an attempt to set up a branch in Australia, and though a foothold was established, in the beginning it was so small and so far away that the project itself seemed quixotic. Okay, so there is an Amway office in Australia, thought some folks back home, but in a practical sense, of what use is it?

The Wright Brothers, it is said, were challenged by a skeptic who thought them little more than tinkerers. "Okay, so it works. But what good is your flying contraption? What will it accomplish?" And they replied, "What good is a new-born child?"

After the first year of that first Australian venture, the baby was alive and well, but many must have wondered, "What good is it?" It was the beginning of Amway's inter-national thrust, which today includes major corporate offices in the Pacific areas of Japan, Taiwan, Hong Kong, and Malaysia, the European countries of Great Britain, Ireland, France, Germany, Belgium, the Netherlands, Switzerland, and Austria, as well as smaller operations in two dozen other countries and territories on four continents. Some company officials predict that by 1990 there will be as many Amway products sold outside the United States as inside.

The decision to try to establish Amway in Australia followed the success of the company in the 1960s in Canada and Puerto Rico. Though Canada is not in any sense "foreign" to an American company, operating there did involve two troublesome aspects which would be encountered in an overseas effort—the need to cope with language differences (in French-speaking Quebec), and the technical problems of sending products across an international border. Opening the business in Puerto Rico provided a test for another of the challenges which are part of foreign expansion—that of shipping products to an area separated by many miles of water.

So both Quebec and Puerto Rico presented some of the difficulties which would have to be overcome for Amway to become an international business, and the rapid growth of the business in those areas emboldened DeVos and Van Andel for the Australian experiment.

As each barrier was reached, it was crossed with surprising lack of difficulty. Language differences were no problem. "Fortunately, money is bilingual," explained a French-speaking leader in Canada. Overseas shipping was handled by use of huge sea containers, which are loaded at the Ada manufacturing plant, shipped by truck or rail to ports on the east or west coast of the United States, and offloaded directly into warehouses in the destination country.

The problem one might expect would create the greatest challenge, that of transplanting this specifically American phenomenon into a different culture, proved to be least difficult of all. It turns out that Amway is not particularly American at all. Whatever its attraction is, it obviously is more common to hardworking, upward mobile, free people everywhere than any national identity or citizenship can be.

Amway is now expanding into international markets at a rate of over one new country per year. As more new areas are reached, the ease of expansion increases. Already Amway materials are being translated into French, Spanish, German, and Dutch for European markets, and into Japanese, Chinese, and Malay for Pacific markets. The addition of Taiwan, for example, in the Pacific area was made much easier by (1) a support staff already in place in that region, (2) materials available in the Chinese language, (3) the ease with which Amway officials could add the island to their Pacific travel itineraries, and (4) the existence of an Amway "presence" among people of that area.

The same process works with the European expansion into Austria, for example, when operations already exist just across the border in Germany. In the race to develop international subsidiaries, it is obviously a case of "them that has, gets." The bigger Amway is, the easier to become bigger still.

Though distributors in overseas markets are far removed geographically from the corporate home base in Michigan, they seem to develop an emotional tie to Ada and the Van Andel–DeVos legend similar to that seen in North America. For some international distributors, a trip to the United States *must* include visits at the Statue of Liberty, Washington, D.C., Disneyland, and Ada, Michigan! It is a rather unlikely choice for a list of can't-miss destinations, but many foreign tourists who are also Amway distributors would sooner skip the Grand Canyon than the Center of Free Enterprise.

Perhaps the biggest single wave of such overseas guests so far was a group of German distributors who visited Ada in the summer of 1984. More than five thousand of them came in a ten-day period. They came in groups of three- to five-hundred each, traveling on charter flights, with each group staying for three days. The first wave was greeted at the Grand Rapids airport by a college marching band and the mayor, along with various Amway brass. (They arrived, coincidentally, on the fortieth anniversary of the D-Day invasion.) It has been estimated that more West Germans visited Amway headquarters in that ten-day period than attended the entire 1984 Olympic Games in Los Angeles later that summer!

That is only one of the many anecdotes which illustrate the surge of Amway vitality and enthusiasm in countries all over the world. In Japan, where the direct-sales tradition is much stronger than in most countries of Europe or in North America, Amway's recruiting rate now shows the steepest climb per capita of any country on the map. A team of Japanese journalists representing two national magazines recently traveled the seven thousand miles to Ada to interview Amway officials about the company and its overseas expansion.

Major new markets to be opened next may include Italy and a still-undisclosed Latin American country. Out there in the future somewhere, say Amway officials, the company is considering many possibilities including, of all places, the People's Republic of China.

What does it all mean, this explosion of international business? In a practical sense, of course, it means vast new markets for Amway products, as well as millions of potential distributors who may be recruited by North Americans through Amway's innovative plan of "international sponsors." But the larger significance may have been expressed by another Amway-watcher several years ago, when the dramatic international expansion was just beginning:

"The spread of Amway into foreign markets is impressive because Amway is exporting more than just a line of household products. It is spreading a way of life which emphasizes free enterprise, a point of view, an approach to one's individual condition in life and what he can do about it. The success of Amway in foreign markets is important because it demonstrates that, for all the Americanism that pervades the rhetoric of the company back home, the basic principles of

Amway are not so much American as they are common to
men and women everywhere. Hard work, sacrifice for a later
reward, a dollar's worth of product for a dollar's price, personal service to customers—those are not uniquely American
principles. They have a broader base than that, and they are
the principles that make Amway work."

.9.

THREE DOZEN AND ONE QUESTIONS ABOUT AMWAY

The more highly visible Amway becomes in the market-place, the more questions are asked about what it is and how it operates. Amway is one of those subjects about which everyone seems to know a little, but very few people know a lot.

The same set of questions is almost sure to pop up whenever the conversation turns to Amway. Getting good answers to Amway questions can be tricky. Whom to ask? The public-relations department of the corporation itself would hardly offer a detached view, and ditto for many of the distributors. It's not that they can't be trusted; it's just that one doesn't expect totally objective answers to tough questions when one's own business is the subject.

Rudolf Flesch, in his classic little book *The Art of Clear Thinking,* offers this warning: "Don't believe grownups who tell you that children love spinach, wives who insist that husbands like pastels and chintz, Democrats who are sure Republicans despise their own candidates, whites who explain that blacks prefer segregation, businessmen who announce that labor wants to get rid of unions, or employers who tell you that small boys love to work."

Seeking answers about Amway from a supposedly disinterested bystander is an even worse way to get reliable information. With the increased media attention given to Amway in the 1980s, it has become decidedly unfashionable *not* to have an opinion on the subject. The average person-on-the-street is likely to be an amateur Amway expert. Just ask. The problem is that their "information" is usually misinformation, and frequently misses the facts by a considerable distance.

Hearing outsiders discuss Amway brings to mind a similar situation described by Ernest Hemingway: "Nobody knew anything about it," he said, "although they all spoke with great positiveness and strategical knowledge."

It has been observed that when the subject turns to Amway, never in the history of human events have so many known so little about so much and been so unwilling to acknowledge it!

Here are some unofficial answers to those questions you've had about Amway, but didn't know whom to ask.

1. Is Amway the Company That Fixes Transmissions?

No. That's Aamco.

2. Does Amway Operate Those Hotels at Airports?

No. That's Amfac.

3. Didn't Amway Get Taken Apart by Mike Wallace on "60 Minutes" a Couple of Years Ago?

Yes and no.

Yes, Amway was the subject of a Mike Wallace investigative report on "60 Minutes" in early 1983. But no, Amway was not "taken apart" on that show. On that point both Amway officials and Wallace himself agree. About the worst that can be said is that Amway underwent the full "60 Minutes" treatment and landed on its feet.

The story of Mike Wallace and Amway is an interesting one. Most Mike Wallace stories are interesting, or at least the public apparently feels they are. In the past decade he has become one of America's best-known media personalities; his show regularly leads the television ratings; and when he wrote a book recently about his experiences, *Close Encounters,* it jumped immediately onto the national bestseller lists.

Mike Wallace is big news, and when he does a "60 Minutes" report on a business or an individual, people notice. In his book, Wallace describes the degree to which his name is associated with the exposure of evil deeds and evildoers. As his reputation for investigative reporting grew, he says, "I kept bumping into people who jumped at the chance to alert me to some scandal or outrage that was ripe for exposure on '60 Minutes.' They would give me vivid accounts of foul deeds and culprits perpetrating them, and urge me to take appropriate action: 'You really should look into this, Mike. It's right up your alley.' "

Wallace's notoriety as the television newsman who goes after the bad guys is so complete that the public has come to assume automatically that to be the focus of "60 Minutes" is tantamount to being indicted and convicted of some terrible sin. Wallace is aware of that problem, and describes as "not-so-funny" the joke that "you know it's going to be a blue Monday when you arrive at your office and find a '60 Minutes' crew there waiting for you." Wallace's staff at the CBS Network offices coined a phrase for the typical reaction to a Wallace interview: "Mike Fright," they called it. The network worked to cultivate this Wallace mystique. As free-lance writer Gary Paul Gates describes it, "CBS management has taken steps to make sure that 'Mike Wallace is here' continues to be recognized as 'the four most dreaded words in the English language.' "

Little wonder, then, that Amway people feared the worst when Wallace came to call. Accustomed as they were to reporters who file superficial stories which distort the Amway picture, they had to decide whether to resist Wallace's attempt to do the story or to cooperate with him and take their chances. They chose to cooperate, and it proved to be a good decision, since the report when it finally appeared was far from being a quick-and-dirty journalistic rip job.

Van Andel and DeVos did their homework. After agreeing to be interviewed on camera by Wallace in their Ada, Michigan, offices, they engaged as a consultant Walter Pfister, a former vice president of ABC News, who came to Ada to prepare them to face Wallace. Currently the owner of the Executive Television Workshop in New York, Pfister performs a similar service for many corporate heads who face potentially hostile television interviews. "I realize how many people are not really prepared for interviews," he explains. "Mike Wallace has spent his whole life learning how to ask questions. Maybe executives should take a day or two learning to answer them."

In addition to interviews with DeVos and Van Andel, the CBS team wished to spotlight one leader from the distributor force, and selected Dexter Yager, a Charlotte, North Carolina, distributor whose Amway organization is one of the largest and most profitable in the history of the company. Yager was also prepped for his contact with Wallace, and like the co-founders proved able to keep his cool and score his points when the interview came.

When the report finally aired in early 1983, its balanced and moderate view of the Amway operation showed that Wallace, whatever his attitude might have been at the outset, had finally concluded that Amway did not deserve the scathing criticism for which "60 Minutes" is famous. The Grand Rapids *Press* described the piece as a "middle-of-the-road view of Amway."

Speaking of the Amway story several months later, Wallace acknowledged that he had begun his investigation with several "preconceived misconceptions" which he had discovered were not true. He told a reporter, "We found their products are good, and that they're not a pyramid operation." Interviewed by late-night radio host Larry King, on a national Mutual Broadcasting show, Wallace was questioned again on the subject, and joked that his attitude was so positive toward the company that "this is going to sound like a commercial for Amway." He described his own expectations of the show: "We thought we would have to do the story without cooperation, but these are classy people. They opened up to us . . . these people are first rate."

Several months later, Wallace was still citing Amway as an example of an open company with nothing to hide. Questioned by Ted Koppel on an ABC television news show, he discussed the tendency some companies have of trying to stonewall the "60 Minutes" crew: "I think a business serves itself much better by being forthcoming, by taking its chances unless it has something it wants to hide. . . . Let me give you examples. The Amway Corporation . . . felt they had something to gain by making the best case that they could. They didn't ask for questions ahead of time, they didn't ask for any special editing privileges. They were forthcoming, they opened their books, they opened their plants to us. And as a result, you can talk to these people, and they'll say, perhaps it wasn't the broadcast that we would have liked to see, but it was fair, it was balanced, it was accurate, and we probably did ourselves good in the long run."

If any doubt remained about where Mike Wallace stands on the legitimacy of the Amway operation, he removed it once and for all in the fall of 1983, when he accepted Amway's invitation to appear as a guest at their Executive Diamond Council in Grand Rapids. He conducted a question-and-answer session with leading distributors, posed for pictures and signed autographs.

If "Mike Wallace is here" are indeed the four most dreaded words in the English language, then perhaps it is true that the ultimate media accomplishment is to face the famous investigator and make a believer out of him. When Mike Wallace comes in, with all his resources and skill, and decides your operation is okay, that's a pretty impressive statement of confidence.

4. Isn't Amway a Pyramid? (I Thought Pyramids Were Illegal Anyway.)

Anytime Amway is discussed, whether on a radio call-in show or around the coffee machine at the office, this question is sure to be raised. Ever since the widely publicized pyramiding scandals of the 1960s, which featured the flamboyant Glenn Turner and his Koscot and "Dare to Be Great" operations, the public has been immediately skeptical about any marketing plan that even vaguely resembles a pyramid.

The question of whether Amway is a pyramid can be answered as a matter of legal definition backed up by court rulings. Yes, pyramids are illegal. No, Amway is not a pyramid. That is not just the personal opinion of Amway people; it is a matter of legal record.

There seems to be little doubt about Amway's non-pyramid status in the legal community, even though that word has not reached some parts of the general public. Edward Bladen is assistant attorney general in charge of the Economic Crime Division in Amway's home state of Michigan. Asked by a Washington *Times* reporter about the Amway operation, he responded: "We have not had any information on record to lead us to believe that they are a pyramid scheme. *In fact, they are one of our staunchest supporters of anti-pyramiding schemes.* They've basically advised legislators these kinds of things shouldn't be done." (emphasis added)

Similarly, an attorney general in Maryland, Steve Sachs, seemed to go out of his way in a recent interview on a Baltimore television show to set the record straight on Amway's status. In a discussion of pyramid operations in his state, Sachs offered this comment: "These are different from some of the fairly heavy commissioned sales arrangements. Amway is one that comes to mind. Now they've been okayed by the courts because ... it's not the same lottery aspect that the pyramid thing does. ... I'm not here to give testimonials

Amway founders and partners Richard M. DeVos and Jay Van Andel pose for an official portrait in the corporation's executive suite.

Amway's advertising in recent years has included television and magazine commercials which feature Bob Hope. Here he entertains an
Amway convention crowd in Kansas City.

Former president Gerald Ford, a native of Grand Rapids, has been a friend of Amway since its earliest days. Here he meets guests at a corporate reception, with Jay Van Andel doing the introductions.

Mike Wallace, of CBS-TV and "60 Minutes," visited with Amway distributors in Grand Rapids after his report on the company in 1983. Here he smiles for the camera with Jerry and Sharyn Webb, of Texas.

An aerial shot of Amway's corporation headquarters and manufacturing facilities in Ada, Michigan.

The final phase of construction of the Amway Grand Plaza Hotel was this high-rise tower, which overlooks the Gerald R. Ford Presidential Museum in Grand Rapids.

Mass rallies which attract thousands of Amway distributors are one of the most colorful features of the Amway operation.

Bernice Hansen *(on the right)*, is a Michigan grandmother who heads one of Amway's largest organizations. She was once named one of America's "ten leading salespersons" by a national publication.

Dick DeVos and Nan Van Andel, the oldest children of Amway's co-founders, have already spent almost ten years each in their careers at the company. Both are vice-presidents.

Amway distributors have contributed over one million dollars in each of the last two Easter Seals telethons. Here Virginia distributors John and Jennie Belle Crowe *(left)* talk on camera with Rich DeVos and entertainer Pat Boone.

President Ronald Reagan addresses a "Salute to Free Enterprise" crowd in Atlanta in 1984, an event sponsored by Amway and the Atlanta Chamber of Commerce. Also seen in the picture are Jay Van Andel *(to Reagan's left)*, and Rich DeVos *(second from left)*.

Part of Amway's Twenty-fifth Anniversary celebration was a concert by the National Symphony Orchestra performed for top distributors at the Kennedy Center in Washington, D.C. Here California distributors Dallas and Betty Beaird stop for a picture at the center.

A group of distributors, in Washington for the 1984 Twenty-fifth Anniversary Celebration, pose at the Capitol Building.

Alexander Haig, former Secretary of State, now serves Amway as a consultant in international affairs. Here he answers questions at a press conference in Grand Rapids with Van Andel and DeVos.

Amway's highest award level for distributors is that of Crown Ambassador. The first to achieve it was this Minnesota couple, Dick and the late Bunny Marks.

Amway of Canada includes almost one hundred thousand distributors, with a major presence in every province. Leading the distributor force in Western Canada are Jim and Sharon Janz of Vancouver *(above)*. French-speaking distributors in the East are led by André and Françoise Blanchard *(below)* of Montreal.

Among the rewards for reaching the level of Direct Distributor is having one's name enshrined in the Hall of Achievement at Amway headquarters. Here, unidentified visitors in a tour group look for their names.

Distributors who reach the "Double Diamond" level are brought to the Ada headquarters for a day in their honor. Here George and Ruth Halsey, accompanied by their sons, tour the plant on "Halsey Day."

A crew shot of the *Enterprise III*, the company's "floating conference room," which operates from Peter Island, the Amway-owned resort in the British Virgin Islands.

Part of Amway's aviation fleet (one 727 is missing from this photo), which shuttles corporate officials and key distributors to and from Grand Rapids.

for any particular company, but Amway is one that's been okayed by the courts. It's not a pyramid scheme. People are buying products, getting value for what they're buying. It has a heavy commission arrangement but that's okay."

To people without legal training, the line between an illegal pyramid and a legitimate marketing plan may seem a thin one. Actually, the characteristics that make a pyramid a pyramid are well defined by a whole set of laws, most of which have been written or at least refined since the Turner scandals gave wide media attention to the problem.

Rodney K. Smith, an attorney and professor of contract law at the University of North Dakota School of Law, explains what a pyramid is in his book *Multilevel Marketing:* "The two primary characteristics of an illegal pyramid are clear. They are: (1) "inventory loading"—the notion that new recruits must purchase a substantial, nonreturnable inventory to get involved in the business, with their sponsor rewarded for the new distributor's purchase of the inventory; and (2) a "headhunting fee"—the notion that the new recruit or distributor is to pay a large sum of money as an entry fee, the sponsor to receive a portion of that fee. The presence of either or both of these factors will generally suffice to label an enterprise as an illegal pyramid."

The most direct clarification of Amway non-pyramid status has come from the courts themselves. When a California court found a company called Figurettes guilty of pyramiding in the late 1970s, the defendants claimed legitimacy by comparing their marketing plan to Amway's. The court flatly refused to accept such a comparison, and in so ruling offered an appraisal of the Amway difference: "Amway had avoided the abuses of a pyramid scheme by (1) not having a headhunting fee . . . (2) making product sales a precondition for receiving the performance bonus . . . (3) buying back unsold inventory . . . and (4) requiring a substantial percentage of products be sold to customers at retail. . . ."

The Federal Trade Commission ruled directly that Amway is not a pyramid in its findings in 1978. After months of hearings and legal inquiry, Judge Timony ruled in favor of Amway in a clear and unambiguous way: "The Amway sales and marketing plan is not a pyramid plan. In less than twenty years, it has built a substantial manufacturing company and an efficient distribution system, which has brought new products into the market. . . . Consumers are benefited by this new source of supply, and have responded by remarkable brand loyalty to Amway products."

Professor Rodney Smith reviews all these cases in his book and reaches this emphatic conclusion: "It is clear that Amway is not and never has been an illegal pyramid scheme."

5. Someone Told Me He Was in Amway and Lost Lots of Money Several Years Ago. Does That Sort of Thing Happen Often?

It is difficult to lose "lots of money" in Amway, by the very nature of the marketing plan. Amway does not sell franchises or allow the initial purchase of large amounts of inventory. The initial cost of a sales kit is only about seventy-five dollars, or, as some of Amway's promotional literature once described it, "about the cost of a new pair of shoes."

One reason for keeping the cost so low is to avoid the very problem this question describes: large losses taken by unsuccessful distributors. It obviously is not in the best interest of the company to have disgruntled former distributors talking about how they lost money in Amway, so for that reason, if for no other, Amway is designed to minimize the chance of that happening.

What Amway cannot control, of course, is the amount of money new distributors spend for things which they hope will help them in their Amway businesses. One former distributor, for example, complained loudly that he had lost several hundred dollars in Amway, though he was active in the business for only a few weeks. The reporter who listened to his story inquired more closely: How could it be possible, he asked, to lose that much money when start-up costs are so low? It turned out that the unhappy former distributor, in his first few days in the business, had rushed out and bought the whole range of video equipment—camera, recorder, playback monitor—apparently with the thought that he would overwhelm his prospects with all that flashy technology.

Within a few weeks, High-Tech Harry had decided not to follow through on his Amway business, but still was left with a closetful of expensive video equipment. Hence his complaint that he had lost a bundle on Amway. Obviously it was not Amway that cost him money, but rather his own proclivity for plunging prematurely into big-ticket sales aids. Most stories of people losing money in an Amway business are variations on this theme.

6. I Read in the Paper That Amway Was Fined Twenty-Five Million Dollars by the Canadian Government. What Was That All About? Is Amway Still Operating in Canada?

Yes, Amway of Canada is still operating, and in fact exceeded its projections in sales and profits in the 1983–84 fiscal year. There are approximately one hundred thousand Amway distributors in Canada, and they account for nearly one hundred million dollars in sales volume annually. After a year of no growth which mirrored the sales slump on the American side, Canadian Amway activity is now growing again.

The twenty-five-million-dollar fine to which you refer was a result of a customs dispute between Amway and Revenue Canada, the branch of the Canadian government which collects tariffs. The dispute was a complicated one which began in the early 1970s, when Amway first began shipping products from its manufacturing plant in Michigan across the international boundary to its distributors in Canada.

Because of Amway's unconventional marketing method, in which the company sells to "direct" distributors, who pass products on to other distributors, the question of how to fix the amount of customs duty to be paid by Amway was not readily answered. Amway paid according to an agreement made with Canadian officials at that time, which the Canadian courts have now ruled is invalid.

By the time all this legal maneuvering was over, tens of millions of dollars were at stake, and the fine, when it was finally levied, was a very large one. Even in Canadian dollars, twenty-five million is plenty. Little wonder the case produced headlines in hundreds of newspapers!

An important point, which some people seem to have missed, is that the legitimacy of the Amway marketing system was never at issue in the case at all. When a headline speaks of Amway incurring such a huge fine, people who read no further might conclude that it is Amway's entire method of operation which was tried and found wanting by the Canadian courts. That is not true. This was a customs case, plain and simple. It had nothing at all to do with pyramids, multilevel sales, truth in advertising, or any other of those more provocative subjects. It was an argument between Amway and Revenue Canada over how much duty to pay, and Amway lost the argument.

Another interesting note on the Canadian affair is that it seems not to have dimmed the luster of the Amway business for Canadian distributors. Soon after the fine was announced, DeVos traveled across Canada on a speaking tour, drawing crowds of thousands of distributors in Vancouver, Winnipeg, Calgary, Toronto, and Montreal. A Grand Rapids reporter traveling with him described his reception as "a hero's welcome." DeVos told the crowds that he came to Canada "because Jay and I are committed to this business. We're committed to Canada. And we're committed to you."

Canadian distributors generally seem to share his attitude that the much-publicized fines were a mere bump in the road. Andre Blanchard is a leading distributor based in

Montreal who feels that the future is bright for Amway in Canada. His distributor organization conducted a special sales promotion just ten days after the fines were announced in Ottawa, and sold $948,000 worth of products in a week. "The consumers are ready to buy our products," he said. "We've been hit every week with some news that was not always positive, but we have found that people don't care, especially when it involves the government. We really don't see any negatives at all!"

7. What Is an Amway Distributor and What Does One of Them Do? How Does the System Actually Work?

A decent answer to that question constitutes what Amway people call "the plan." It takes an hour or more for a distributor to explain it properly, and they all seem to do it a bit differently. For someone not in Amway to attempt an explanation of how it all works is like having a tone-deaf kid explain the subtleties of Bach. But, with apologies all around, here is a brief outline:

Basically, Amway distributors do two things: They sell Amway products to their friends, neighbors, and other retail customers—and they recruit other people to do the same.

Selling the products is simple. The distributor has a product list of about three hundred and fifty items to offer the customer. These products are made by Amway, usually come in concentrated form, and most are everyday items for home and personal care that everyone uses. The distributor makes an immediate income on all the products he or she sells, usually about 30 percent of the retail price.

The second activity—that of recruiting other people to become distributors—is called "sponsoring." Under some conditions, the distributor may receive a bonus on the sales volume of anyone he or she brings into the business. There is no money to be made merely for recruiting a new distributor, but if that distributor actually goes to work and generates sales, the company pays a bonus to the sponsor for supplying him with products and training him in sales techniques. One can make a potentially large income if there are large numbers of people whom he or she has sponsored working actively in the Amway business.

Successful Amway distributors are constantly working not only to sell products themselves, but to urge other people to "go thou and do likewise." Amway operates a string of warehouses across the U.S. and Canada called Regional Distribution Centers, and products are shipped from these points to the distributors, who take them personally to the customer. It is strictly a cash-as-you-go proposition; the customer pays cash to the distributor, and the distributor pays cash to the company.

The world of Amway has its own vocabulary. For the uninitiated reader, here is a quick and handy glossary:

Sponsor   To "sponsor" another individual is to bring her into the business by persuading her to sign an application and become a distributor herself. Jack receives no money for sponsoring Jill, but agrees to train, supply, and motivate her, and receives a bonus from the corporation based on Jill's sales volume as she develops her business.

Leg   Every new distributor whom Jack sponsors becomes a "leg" in his organization. When Jack sponsors Jill, she is only one of his legs, along with anyone whom Jill might ultimately sponsor. So the number of legs Jack has is the same as the number of people he has personally sponsored.

Personal group   All the distributors whom Jack has sponsored, plus those whom *they* have sponsored, and so on, up to the first Direct Distributor. To say that Joe is in Jack's personal group doesn't mean that Jack is his boss or any such thing as that. It simply means that Joe is somewhere in the "family tree."

Direct Distributor   Becoming a Direct Distributor is the first major goal in the Amway business. That level is reached when a distributor and his or her group generate sales of approximately $10,000 a month for three straight months. (The exact dollar amount changes as it is periodically adjusted for inflation.) When Jill becomes a Direct Distributor, she purchases her products directly from the corporation rather than from Jack.

Show the plan   To "show the plan" is to explain the Amway sales and marketing system to a prospective distributor. Jack may show the plan by using a marking board, flip chart, slides, or for that matter by writing on the back of a place mat at an all-night restaurant.

Opportunity meeting   Any meeting in which a distributor brings a number of prospects together to show the plan to all of them simultaneously.

Break off a Direct   When Jack sponsors Jill into the business, and Jill reaches the level of Direct Distributor, Jack is said to have "broken off a Direct Distributor." In other words he has helped a distributor whom he sponsored to reach the level of Direct Distributor. The corporation pays a monthly bonus to Jack for helping Jill reach this level, based on 3 percent of her total sales volume.

Diamond   Amway gives a series of award pins to Direct Distributors who break off Directs or reach other goals. The "diamond" pin is one of these, and is given when a distributor breaks off Directs in six different legs. Obviously there is more than a lapel pin at stake here. Along with the pins go cash bonuses and other incentives. These pin awards, in ascending order, are as follows: RUBY, EMERALD, DIAMOND, DOUBLE DIAMOND, TRIPLE DIAMOND, CROWN, and

CROWN AMBASSADOR. Informally, these pin levels
come to represent ranks in the distributor hierarchy;
one's level of success is defined by the pin worn.

8. Much Is Said About the Potential to Make Big Money in Amway. How Can There Be that Much Money in Soap?

Yes, there is big money in the soap and detergent industry—
as in the cosmetics industry and other consumer lines which
make up Amway's product list. These are multibillion-dollar
industries with traditionally large markups from the manufacturing cost of the item to the retail price which the consumer expects to pay. The sale of oven cleaners and lipstick
is not as glamorous as big-ticket industries such as automo-
biles and real estate, and thus the financial potential of a
"soap business" is sometimes underestimated. But the little
pieces of money add up to big ones; there's gold in them
shampoo bottles!

The manufacturer's problem is the high cost of getting the
consumer to buy his or her product over Product X. The vast
number of brand-name products on the grocery store shelf
creates a highly competitive marketplace. A shopper needing
a simple tube of toothpaste faces a wall of nearly identical
products; there may be a dozen different brands from which
to choose. Since it is virtually impossible for the manufacturer to offer a truly new, innovative toothpaste, shoppers
usually select on the basis of name-brand recognition. They
buy those labels which they find familiar. That means advertising—and lots of it—if the product is to build and
maintain a sizable share of the marketplace.

Advertising is expensive. To mount an effective campaign
on a national basis, tens of millions of dollars must be poured
into television commercials and print ads, and this must be
repeated for each individual product or group of products.
Commercials which tout a particular shaving cream have
little impact on the name-recognition of a hair spray, even
though both come from the same company. American Air-

lines, for example, has only a single service to sell, so all its advertising dollars can focus on that one service. In contrast, manufacturers of home and personal care products must duplicate the advertising expenditures of each of their products if they are to compete in the retail store.

In a media age when thirty seconds of television time can cost a hundred thousand dollars, this all adds up to a very expensive proposition. An industry giant such as Procter and Gamble might spend as much as five hundred *million* dollars a year on television advertising alone. Most companies accept such large expenditures as an unavoidable cost of doing business. The major companies merely figure advertising expenses into the price of the product, so that a substantial chunk of every dollar Sam Suburbanite pays for shoe polish actually is spent to convince him he should buy that particular brand.

Amway's marketing strategy contrasts sharply with this conventional approach. Basically, the Amway distributor takes the place not only of the retail store, but of the advertising agent as well. Amway Corporation does a modest amount of television and print advertising, but has never relied on it as a primary means of gaining market share. Instead, by taking products directly to the consumer, Amway bypasses any head-to-head competition with other brands, eliminating the need for massive infusions of advertising cash. That money is instead paid directly to the distributors. After all, they deserve it, the reasoning goes, since it is they, not a Madison Avenue ad agency, who have created the demand for Amway products. These payments are made to the distributors according to a rather elaborate formula of bonuses which are part of the Amway "plan."

So the big money earned by some Amway distributors is real, and it is not spun from thin air. The money is available because the industry itself is geared to pay a large percentage of its gross income back into its delivery system. In Amway's delivery system, money which might otherwise flow to television networks and ad agencies flows instead to its distributors.

9. Why Are Amway Products So Expensive?

Many Amway products are sold in concentrated form, which makes them more convenient for the distributor to store and deliver, but which also gives the misleading impression that the products are overpriced. Amway Corporation insists that its products, when compared on a cost-per-use basis, are no more expensive than those of its competitors, and the evidence supports that claim.

Obviously, a box of detergent which washes four times as many clothes as does a box of comparable size is a bargain even if it costs twice as much. When cost comparisons are made on that basis, Amway's prices are competitive, and in some cases lower than similar brands. A casual shopper may not spend the time to take into account the concentrated form in which the product is delivered, which is one reason companies which sell their products on the supermarket shelf are reluctant to produce concentrated goods, despite the many advantages which concentration offers both the customer and the company. With Amway's system of in-home marketing, the cost-per-use principle can be explained and demonstrated.

Perhaps the most convincing evidence that Amway's prices are competitive is the company's track record as a viable, growing business for twenty-five years. People are buying Amway products to the tune of a billion dollars a year, and that kind of sales performance could not be maintained if its prices were consistently higher than the competition.

10. Why Can't I Buy Amway Products in the Grocery Store, Like I Buy Everything Else?

From its beginning in 1959, Amway has been committed to its posture as a direct-sales company. Direct sales offers an alternative to the traditional system of delivering goods to the consumer through retail stores. Instead, the individual distributor develops customers and sells directly to them.

Having begun in this fashion, Amway vows it is committed to continue, since to begin placing products in retail stores would obviously undercut its own distributors, who have cultivated customers' loyalty over the years. If Jane Doe introduces her neighbor to a particular Nutrilite (i.e., Amway) food supplement, she should be able to continue to sell to that neighbor without having to compete with her own supplier, Amway Corporation, which might be selling the same product through a local supermarket.

Since its products have earned a good reputation among consumers, the profits Amway might earn by selling through stores are potentially great, but the company sticks with its direct-sales system, it says, as a matter of principle. The attitude is similar to the country-boy code of "dancing with who brung you to the dance." In a press interview on the occasion of Amway's twenty-fifth anniversary in late 1984, Van Andel and DeVos indicated that the distributor-based marketing plan is the one absolutely unchangeable element of the Amway system.

"Amway has a commitment to this selling method and to the people who are involved with and are selling our merchandise," Van Adel was quoted. "Everything we are looking at [for the future] is geared around how we can help them to become more successful, not around alternative ways of marketing the products."

So the public is not likely to see Amway products on the supermarket shelf, no matter how popular they are with consumers.

11. What About These "Mass Rallies" Amway Has? I've Heard They Get People Together in These Revival-Type Meetings Just to Manipulate Them and Whip Up Their Emotions.

Yes, they have "mass rallies." Boy, do they ever have mass rallies! Large meetings in convention halls and arenas, some-

times involving thousands of people, are an important part
of the Amway operation.

These rallies are the first—and sometimes the only—facet
of the Amway phenomenon which outsiders see, and are certainly the aspect of the Amway business which the press
seems to find most interesting. When several thousand people get together in the same place at the same time, it creates
the kind of visually appealing "hook" which television and
news photographers, in particular, find almost irresistible. As
a result, the focus of most stories about Amway over the
years has been the spectacular mass meetings which the company and its distributors conduct.

These rallies have been compared to everything from the
Nuremberg pageants in Nazi Germany to the old-fashioned
revival meetings of fundamentalist Christian evangelists.
They are usually described in the press as being intensely
emotional, almost as if some sort of semi-hypnotic brainwashing occurs, and the concern is sometimes voiced that in
the supercharged environment of these rallies people are
manipulated into doing things they would otherwise find
objectionable.

This view of the Amway rally as some sort of sinister force
doesn't fit the facts. The meetings can be colorful and at
times even boisterous, and a person attending for the first
time might suffer from sensory overload compounded by
culture shock. It is a bit unnerving to find oneself surrounded
by hundreds of people having that much fun and expressing
that much excitement without use of intoxicating spirits or
other chemical aid. But the comparisons to religious revival
meetings and mass brainwashing sessions do not describe the
mood and tone very well. The atmosphere is not so much
"intense" as it is "celebratory." These people are having fun;
strange as it seems, they are simply enjoying themselves im-
mensely while conducting a business meeting.

The suggestion that Amway people are emotionally manipulated in these meetings also appears unfounded. "Hey,
look," a distributor responded to that criticism, "these are

not illiterate primitives we're talking about, or a coupla thousand teeny-boppers at a rock concert. These are mature, intelligent, sensible men and women in this crowd. We just enjoy getting together, sharing our dreams and our goals with each other, and expressing our excitement about life. Most of us have other jobs where we have to be more restrained, and it's kinda fun to get together like this and let our hair down a little bit. People are too inhibited about their feelings anyway. In Amway meetings, we just feel free to be ourselves more than most people do. It's like going to a good football game. Everybody screams and hollers and jumps up and down, but it doesn't mean they're being manipulated by the cheerleaders, does it? They're just having a good time."

To compare the crowd at an Amway rally to that at a college football game is probably more accurate than the analogy of a religious revival meeting. The behavior of a crowd at a college football game is absurd on the face of it. Here is a situation in which tens of thousands of people gather to watch a handful of young men take turns carrying a large piece of brown leather back and forth across a plot of grass. The boys who engage in this peculiar activity are strangers to the thousands of people who come to watch them play. The outcome of their little contest will in no way affect the spectators' daily lives; it is merely a game, unrelated to how much money the spectators make, what kind of homes they live in, or any other aspect of their circumstances or well-being after the game is over.

Yet these thousands of people, most of them well-educated and reasonably intelligent, will for three hours engage in behavior that verges on being certifiably psychotic. They will scream and laugh; they will vilify referees and opposing players; they will rise to their feet periodically, not to see better but to contain the suspense; they will break into wild fits of joy and turn to one another to slap hands and embrace. On occasion they will sing songs with strange lyrics or chant silly ditties, or jump up and down rhythmically, arms flung into the air, in something called a "wave." They will go from euphoric, thigh-wacking, whooping shouts of joy to bitter, angry booing—and back again—in a moment's time.

These are not teenagers or members of remote island tribes who will do these things, but stockbrokers, physicians, heads of large corporations, bankers, PTA presidents, serious-minded businessmen and women, professors, judges, pillars of a hundred communities, and even an occasional CPA.

Compared to this picture, the most boisterous Amway rally seems sedately reassuring!

In one of Agatha Christie's novels, a character asks another who has just described a peculiar sight: "Don't you think you're being rather absurd?" "Yes, I do," she responds; "If this was written down, it would look absurd. But then so many absurd things are true, aren't they?"

12. Is Amway a Christian Movement of Some Sort?

This question is asked so often that the corporation has developed and distributed an official answer to it: "Corporations are not people and cannot be Christian or non-Christian. Amway's co-founders are both members of the Christian Reformed Church, a conservative Protestant Christian church of Dutch Calvinist background, headquartered in Grand Rapids, Michigan. Each has been active as an elder in the church and on various boards and committees. Their religious convictions are made evident by the ethical principles on which the corporation is run. They also have convictions regarding Sunday observance, so Amway factories are closed on Sundays, the truck fleet does not run on Sunday, and no company sales meetings or other business activities are conducted on Sundays. The co-founders do not use the corporate platform or media to promote their particular religious beliefs except in the broad ethical and moral sense. They have taken special care to make sure that persons of any religious belief feel welcome as Amway distributors and employees."

That such a careful public statement should be necessary indicates the degree to which the general public perceives Amway as being religiously aligned with conservative Christianity. The corporation is obviously anxious to avoid being tagged with a sectarian label which might limit sales or discourage non-Christian persons from becoming distributors. The record shows that Amway's reassurances to non-Christian distributors are backed by an active attempt to broaden its socioreligious base.

Though the majority of Amway distributors are members of Christian churches, at least in the United States and Canada, the company attracts large numbers of distributors who are Jewish, Buddhist, or simply not religiously identified in any fashion whatever. Though they clearly represent a minority of the distributor force, as they do in the general population, these Amway people indicate that they do not feel any particular discomfort with the image Amway has in some quarters as a company with a Christian orientation.

13. In My Town It Seems That Half the People I Know Are Getting Into Amway. If Everybody Gets in, Who Is Going to Be Left to Buy the Stuff?

Experts in the field of multilevel marketing call this the "saturation" question. What happens if everybody gets in? It seems a logical concern. Anyone with a calculator and a working knowledge of seventh-grade math can figure out that if there are one million distributors, and each of them sponsors a new distributor each week, there will be two million of them next week, four million the week after that, and sixteen million by the end of the month. In the second month things begin to pick up. There should be sixty-four million distributors by the middle of the month, one hundred twenty-eight million a week after that, and by the end of the second month every adult in the U.S. and Canada will be a card-carrying Amwayer, with several million empty slots left over.

So much for mathematics. The reality is entirely different from what might be predicted by a statistician with a slide rule. Those who fear that it is too late to get into a multilevel sales operation because any day now the world is likely to be saturated with Amway distributors fail to take into account the element of human nature.

How will Amway distributors make money if everybody gets into Amway? It is an interesting hypothetical question, but it makes about as much sense as the one which comedian Dave Gardner constantly asked in the early 1960s: "What will all the preachers do if the Devil gets religion?" One is about as likely to happen as the other.

In the analysis of Amway's operation undertaken by the Federal Trade Commission in 1975–78, the question of saturation was addressed specifically. The judge heard testimony from attorneys who argued that the danger of saturation posed a threat to new distributors coming into the business. Amway's attorneys of course argued otherwise. All the available evidence on both sides of the question was introduced, and the judge's final ruling emphatically concluded that the problem of saturation is in practice not a problem at all.

His official statement included the following observations: "The witnesses whom I have heard and find credible . . . had no difficulty sponsoring new distributors during the relevant time. . . . The facts in this record do not show that Amway distributors in any market were unable to recruit new distributors or to sell Amway products because of any inherent defect in the Amway Sales and Marketing Plan." The judge further quoted a marketing analyst who had testified during the hearing to the effect that complaints about saturation can generally be attributed to other problems such as personal discouragement or lack of effort by the distributor.

The most telling comment from the judge came near the end of his thorough, carefully researched statement: "It is relatively unlikely that the available supply of potential Amway distributors will be exhausted in any particular area." In other words, the hypothetically dangerous problem of market saturation turns out to have little meaning on a practical level.

Why? As Amway points out, for all its rapid growth and billion-dollar size, it still accounts for a tiny share of the overall marketplace—perhaps less than 3 percent. Its product line of approximately three hundred and fifty items covers such a wide range of items that, with expansion into new product areas, it seems unlikely to increase that percentage anytime soon.

The fear that the distributor force itself will expand geometrically with such speed that no prospects will remain seems equally unfounded. The reality is that most distributors do not attempt to sponsor anyone at all, and even in its periods of most rapid growth the Amway distributor force has never grown fast enough even to keep up with the growth of the general population.

An excellent explanation of why the saturation question is a paper tiger is offered by attorney Rodney K. Smith in *Multilevel Marketing*. His reasons are summarized below:

1. The population of the country continues to grow.

2. The opportunity to sponsor people in other geographic areas reduces the danger of a particular area becoming saturated. A person living in Oregon can sponsor a friend in Arkansas and work with him or her effectively because of the way the Amway plan operates. As a result, there are cases in which several distributors living in the same small town each have hundreds of people in their Amway businesses.

3. Amway is now doing business in forty countries and territories, and U.S. and Canadian distributors are able to sponsor internationally through an arrangement in the Amway plan. With this feature, the potential field for sponsoring expands immediately into literally hundreds of millions of homes around the world. Many North American distributors already have stories to tell of branches of their business growing in Japan, Germany, Australia, and so on.

4. Many prospects who turn down the Amway opportunity the first time they see it get aboard after a second look.

5. The dropout rate of Amway, often cited as a negative factor, actually serves to keep the pool of potential distributors large. There are many examples of distributors who succeeded in the business on their second time around.

6. Many young people entering the work force for the first time are surprised to learn that the income from the entry-level jobs available to them is not great enough to finance their high lifestyle expectations. Having fewer resources than older people, this growing segment of the population is unusually apt to find direct sales attractive.

7. Middle-aged and older people also respond well to the opportunities of multilevel marketing when they realize their retirement benefits are likely to be inadequate. Smith cites an example of a couple who got into Amway at the age of sixty-two and built an annual income in excess of $100,000 in less than three years.

8. A gradual weakening of the status-related objections to the Amway business should result in higher sponsoring rates for those distributors approaching prospects in the last half of the 1980s.

For the reasons which Smith cites, as well as others, the problem of saturation seems not to pose a practical threat to Amway's growth or to the likelihood of success of any particular distributor.

14. I Understand That Half the People Who Get Into Amway Get Out Their First Year. Is This True, and if It Is, What Accounts for the 50 Percent Retention Rate?

True. Roughly half the people who become Amway distributors drop out within a year—that is, they choose not to renew their distributorships at the beginning of the next fiscal year.

There are several considerations which help to put that figure into perspective.

First, 50 percent is not a high attrition level compared to other direct-sales companies; some such companies have much lower retention rates. According to *Working Woman* magazine Avon, for example, has a 150 percent annual turnover rate. Among companies which have a similar structure and marketing plan, Amway's turnover is considered moderate.

Second, the low cost of becoming an Amway distributor affects its nonrenewal rate. Easy come, easy go. The individual who decides to give Amway a try today can change his or her mind tomorrow without worrying too much about losing money. When seventy-five dollars gets you in, there is very little incentive to stay in merely to protect your investment. It has been suggested that Amway increase the initial cost of becoming a distributor for just this reason, but DeVos and Van Andel are determined to keep the business within reach of individuals who have lots of desire but little capital. The concept of offering an opportunity which anyone can afford is deeply rooted in the company's tradition, and the policy is unlikely to change even though it increases attrition percentages.

Third, people who leave the Amway distributor force generally do so with little hostility toward the company or regret at having tried and failed. They don't leave mad; they just leave. As long as this holds true, Amway officials say, they will continue to be unconcerned about retention rates. For most people who get into and out of Amway, the departure is something of a no-fault divorce: we just weren't right for each other so let's go our separate ways.

A survey of nonrenewing distributors—conducted by an independent firm though commissioned by Amway—verifies the view that Amway dropouts usually leave amicably enough. The reasons offered for having left Amway were in almost every case unrelated to satisfaction or dissatisfaction with the business itself. Personal reasons were usually cited, with respondents frequently vaguely expressing that they might try it again later.

The notion that a former Amway distributor is an angry man or woman with a basement full of unsold and unusable products is clearly a fictitious one. In this particular survey,

former distributors were asked how many products they still
had on hand, and not one of the 250 persons polled had as
much as one hundred dollars' worth of stock remaining.
Eighty percent had less than twenty dollars' worth. And
when asked if they would like Amway to buy back whatever
products were still there, 249 out of 250 declined, saying they
would rather keep the products for their own personal use.

Fourth, distributors who fail to renew often sign up again
later. In fact, nearly 20 percent of all new applications for
distributorships come from people who have been in the
business before—a figure which is growing in recent years.
The development of a profitable distributorship seems to be
a matter of random timing in many cases; an individual's
marital and family situation, degree of happiness in a full-
time job, and personal sense of need and ambition all shift
from time to time, and people who are poor prospects for
Amway success at one time in their lives may be good prospects at another time.

Fifth, Amway accepts new distributors on a whosoever-
will-let-him-come basis. There is no attempt to screen applicants as to their suitability for the business, and this obviously increases attrition rates. There is an axiom among
college admissions officers that "an open door is a revolving
door," a principle which operates with Amway's traditional
open-door policy. The company has been criticized for this
approach, but insists that only a totally nonrestrictive policy
provides the open-ended opportunity which is such an essential part of the American dream.

15. Let's Say, for the Sake of Argument, That Amway Corporation Treats Its Distributors Very Well in 1985. But How Do I Know They Won't Change the Deal Now That the Whole Operation Has Gotten So Big?

The best argument against the likelihood of their changing the plan is Amway's twenty-five-year history. In that
entire period, every change in the marketing system has re-

sulted in more benefits, bonuses, or incentives for the distributor force. There has never been a reduction in any of the income-producing elements of the plan for distributors. As DeVos and Van Andel like to say, every Amway distributor is a volunteer, and if the corporation ever treats its volunteers badly, it is out of business.

Another protection against the possibility of future abuse of the distributor force is the existence of the Amway Distributors Association board of directors. This is a board consisting of Van Andel, DeVos, and nine distributors (in Canada, five) who are elected annually at a distributors' convention. This board meets regularly to preview and review the constant flow of onstream corrections which are necessary to make an evolving company like Amway grow. Though the board has no final authority over company policy—that remains in the hands of the owners—it provides an important means of advice and input from the distributor force directly to the top level of corporate management.

Given the unusual interdependence of the company and its distributor force, it is highly unlikely that any arbitrary change in the Amway marketing plan which would negatively affect distributors would be made without consent of the A.D.A. board.

16. I Read Somewhere That DeVos and Van Andel are among the Wealthiest Men in America. Just How Wealthy Are They?

Who knows? Maybe nobody knows, not even DeVos and Van Andel. One thing for sure: if they know, they aren't telling. It is one of the peculiarities of the very rich that they are not being coy when they profess ignorance of their personal net worth; they genuinely have trouble knowing with any precision what the numbers are. Both men have been asked this question from time to time and invariably state that it is private information on which they prefer not to comment.

Such a desire for fiscal privacy has not prevented the press from speculating on what the figures might be, however. Both men appear annually in the *Forbes* magazine listing of the nation's four hundred wealthiest citizens, most recently appearing about midway down the list. *Forbes* puts the net worth of each man at about two hundred and fifty million dollars. *Fortune* magazine once published an even higher figure, estimating the range at three hundred to five hundred million. In both cases, Van Andel and DeVos seem unwilling to dignify the guesswork by commenting on it. They obviously think it's none of our business.

17. For Someone Who Wants to Make a Career of It, Wouldn't It Be Better to Get Into a New Company Similar to Amway, One In Which I Can Get in on the Ground Floor Where the Big Money Can Still Be Made?

A beguiling proposition, that is. Get in on the ground floor while the big money is still lying around to be scooped up. And it follows that Amway, being the creaky old man of multilevel-sales companies at the age of twenty-five, is no longer a place for ambitious beginners to get their start.

The problem with this logic is that any multilevel deal is only as good for one distributor as it is for every other distributor who might follow him or her into the business. If doing well in a multilevel venture requires joining at or near the company's inception, the whole deal eventually collapses because there will be no incentive for anyone to get involved two or five or ten years down the road. So after the "ground floor" is occupied, people quit getting in, and when people quit getting in, the growth and momentum of the entire operation stops.

In Amway, the basic profit formula, the schedule of bonuses and commissions, is the same for everyone who gets into the business, whenever that may be. Every floor is as much the ground floor as any other, and that is what keeps intact the long-term viability of the company.

There is about multilevel sales a misconception that Jack

gets a certain slice of the profits, then Jack brings in Jill, who gets a slightly thinner slice, then Jill brings in Joe, whose slice is a bit less yet, then Joe sponsors Jean, whose slice of the action is even thinner still. The idea is that the further away from the "top" you get, the more people are above you taking a little piece of your action. This is similar to the misconception that in Amway someone else makes money off your work. If that were true, the strategy of joining a young company on the "ground floor" would be a logical one. But that is not the way Amway, or any other soundly structured multilevel company, operates.

In Amway, the money one distributor makes as a result of sponsoring another distributor does not come *out of* that person's profits, but rather is paid by Amway Corporation out of its corporate profits. Every distributor dips into the corporate pot according to the same percentages as any other.

18. Do Most People Leave Their Regular Jobs to Go to Work as Amway Distributors?

No. Some do, but most don't. Amway is designed to be a part-time business at the outset, with the capacity to grow into a full-time one. Amway leaders recommend that new distributors stay with their existing jobs until they have built large and steady businesses, and very few ignore that advice.

The nature of the business is such that it can easily be managed while continuing most other jobs or professions. It also is unlikely to produce enough income in the first few months to offset the distributor's regular wages or salary from the other job. Amway does not work well for the quick-buck artist. Some second-income deals load profits on the front end in hopes of attracting more recruits. Amway is not structured in this fashion; to the contrary, the work of an Amway distributor tends to accrue as the distributor stays involved, with income potentially growing geometrically as he or she stays with it.

While not designed to be full-time immediately, an Amway business grows into a full-time career for many people. One of the most commonly cited reasons for entering Amway is job dissatisfaction. There are obviously millions of people out there who do not enjoy their jobs, for whatever reasons, and see in Amway an opportunity to replace their incomes and pursue Amway on a full-time career basis.

It is a matter of record that Amway delivers on that promise for thousands of people. The company has no statistics on how many of its distributors are full-time, but the number is substantial. The company prefers to emphasize the fact that Amway can be tailor-made to any situation, part-time or full-time. For the majority of distributors, it serves as a supplement to their regular incomes.

19. Why Do Amway Distributors Act as if They Don't Want People to Know What They Are Selling? I Had a Fellow Ask Me to Take a Look at a New Business of His, but He Wouldn't Tell Me What It Was. It Turned Out to Be Amway. Why the Big Secret?

Like most good salespeople, Amway distributors feel they have a very attractive proposition to make. They believe the arguments in favor of your becoming an Amway distributor can be very convincing if given a fair chance of being heard.

The thing that often gets in the way of their ability to convince *you* of that is those preconceived ideas about Amway which you might bring to the situation. Amway is one of those businesses that most people have heard about—one survey puts the national percentage at over 85 percent—but few people genuinely understand. The Amway distributor wants a chance to explain his or her business to you without interference from that fragment of information or misinformation which you may have picked up somewhere else.

The solution for many Amwayers seeking to recruit new

business partners is to get their prospects to agree to hear the whole concept without telling them at the outset what the name of the company is. That way, they figure, the prospect is more likely to have an open mind about Amway from the beginning.

So the scenario often follows the pattern which your question suggests. "I'd like to tell you about a way you can make some extra money," says the distributor. "Well, okay, what's the name of the company?" asks the prospect. "Why don't you wait until I tell you how it works first," says the distributor. And the stage is set for the distributor to "show the plan" without the prospect reaching premature conclusions based on something he heard about Amway on the street somewhere.

This method of getting the prospect's openminded attention until the presentation of the Amway plan is completed is fairly common. Amway people call it the "curiosity approach" because it relies upon the natural curiosity of prospects to counteract the possibility of their rejecting Amway before they understand how it works.

Amway Corporation, and virtually all the top distributor leaders, caution their people against the temptation to stretch curiosity into outright deception. Such abuses do occasionally occur, though not so much in Amway as in other multilevel companies.

In this scenario prospects are not merely tantalized, they are misled. "Hey, let's go bowling Friday night," says the XYZ salesman. "Okay, fine," says the unsuspecting friend. But when the friend shows up on Friday night, wearing a casual shirt and carrying a bowling ball, he is taken not to Sunshine Lanes but to a meeting room in a local motel. "I thought we were going bowling," protests the prospect. "Just kidding," says the distributor. "As you can see, this is not a bowling alley, and you are now going to hear about my new business whether you want to or not."

Needless to say, this approach is considered bad form by Amway leaders, and it rarely occurs. But it has happened.

Why should a company as successful as Amway require any sort of protective camouflage to be introduced to prospective distributors? Apparently because there are many people who misunderstand what it is, and are genuinely surprised, once they have heard the whole thing explained, at how widely the facts about Amway differ from their earlier opinions about it.

"I don't mind when someone really understands what Amway is, and decides not to do it," one distributor stated. "But I hate to see people turn it down based on some crazy idea about it they heard somewhere that's not even true."

The feeling that the general public is largely misinformed about Amway is apparently well-founded. For some reason Amway is unusually susceptible to this problem. Perhaps because of the familiar sound of the name, perhaps because the multilevel-marketing concept is itself fairly new and not well understood, perhaps because there are so many Amway distributors who conduct their business in so many varied ways—who knows the reason why Amway has more than its share of rumors and misconceptions to combat? But the reality for the ambitious distributor is that millions of people *think* they know more about Amway than they actually do.

Amway distributors are not without a sense of humor in this regard. The folklore of the organization is replete with tales of self-appointed Amway experts who talk about the business in ways that reveal their ignorance.

There is the stockbroker in Denver who tells his Amway-distributor client that he has followed the Amway stock on the New York Stock Exchange and recommends it. (It is not listed on the stock exchange.) Or the prospect at an Amway meeting who tells the people sitting nearby that his old college buddy from the University of Minnesota did so well that he is now President of Amway. (DeVos would be surprised to hear that.) Or the cabdriver in Dallas who announces to his passengers that the Adolphus Hotel is owned by Amway. (No such thing.) Or the business editor of a Pittsburgh newspaper who describes the trouble his friend had while "selling Amway" during World War II. (The company was founded in 1959) . . . and so on. The collection of stories is a large one.

With such a large amount of Amway misinformation floating around, it makes good sense to try to get a friend to agree to hear the whole story. This is basically what the "curiosity approach" is all about, and distributors who use it properly report that their prospects do not object to it.

20. I Am Told That Amway Is Primarily a Tax Shelter, and as Such Is in Trouble With the IRS. True or Untrue?

An Amway distributorship is not designed to be a tax shelter. It is designed to be a business, potentially even a big business, which produces big profits for the distributor. A tax shelter typically offers not big profits but big losses—at least on paper—and losses are emphatically *not* what Amway is about.

On the other hand, running an Amway business, like any other, requires the outlay of certain expenses, and those can be legitimately deducted from one's income tax bill. Successful Amway distributors are usually shrewd businessmen and women, and quite naturally seek legal advice on how to take best possible advantage of those wild and crazy Internal Revenue Service regulations.

There is nothing un-American about using every honest loophole which the tax code offers. Unfortunately for the average person who earns income in salary or wages, there are very few legitimate tax write-offs which apply. To the owner of a private business, however, there is a much wider range of legal provisions by which one's tax bill might be reduced. Amway distributors, of course, own their own private businesses.

The pipefitter who has his income taxes withheld from his paycheck each week incurs no deductible business expense, and has no room to maneuver when it comes time to pay

Uncle Sam. If this same pipefitter gets into Amway, he is suddenly in a totally different tax situation insofar as his Amway income is concerned. He does incur business expenses; he does have room to maneuver; and for the first time he has opened up to him some of the tax advantages which the IRS code makes available to the white-collar businessperson but not to the blue-color wage earner.

That doesn't exactly make Amway a tax shelter, but it can be a very welcome opportunity for the pipefitter.

The IRS has no complaint with Amway Corporation, nor indeed with any particular Amway distributor who operates according to its rules. The perception that Amway is "in trouble with the IRS" probably stems from a series of hearings conducted in early 1982 by a subcommittee of the Ways and Means Committee of the U.S. House of Representatives. The hearings were held to investigate possible abuses of tax laws by distributors from various direct-sales companies, and resulted in a major story in *The Wall Street Journal* that was picked up by many local newspapers around the country.

The hearings revealed some titillating examples of the way a few individuals had apparently joined Amway not in a good-faith effort to build a business, but rather to use the Amway name as a personal tax scam to offset other income. According to the *Journal*, one taxpayer who had only $718 in business income claimed deductions of $11,391, including some $7500 for auto expenses and entertaining people in his home. Another taxpayer reported that he had earned only $3600 in Amway, but deducted over $14,000 in expenses against the $52,000 paycheck from his regular job.

Examples such as these obviously come from the tax returns of people who use Amway as a tax dodge, not from distributors whose businesses are earning, rather than losing, large amounts of money. But for the truly creative bookkeeper, the possibilities are endless. One tax return showed that the family pet was listed as a watchdog to guard Amway products, and thus an entire year of dogfood costs was deducted as business expense!

Amway Corporation was understandably unhappy about

the publicity given to these cases of excessive deductions, and has worked to distance itself from the idea that an Amway distributorship is designed to shelter taxes. Van Andel appeared before the Ways and Means subcommittee to testify about the company's efforts to discourage such abuses, and also met with IRS Commissioner Roscoe Egger to discuss the problem and seek ways to counter it.

With a general population which seems increasingly unhappy with the tax laws in general and the IRS in particular, it is not surprising that those who are in a position to slide through tax loopholes are doing so with greater boldness and sophistication. There is nothing illegal about that as long as the loophole game is played according to the rules. Legitimate business deductions for individuals in private business are part of it.

So, while Amway is not a tax shelter, it does get thousands of individuals who have never had a chance to play before into the tax-reduction ballgame. As long as they understand the rules and follow them, not even the IRS will object.

21. Is the Name "Amway" a Contraction for "American Way"?

No. This is commonly believed to be true, but Amway attorneys insist that the word Amway is simply a coined tradename. Undoubtedly the word must have been inspired to some degree by the phrase "American way," at least subliminally, considering the patriotic impulses of the co-founders and many distributors.

But the disclaimer must be taken seriously, in light of the company's willingness to move into international markets without changing or modifying the name. "The American Way of Japan," for example, is a nonsensical expression and would hardly be used by a company as pragmatic in its operation as Amway. For that reason, if for no other, the corporation's statement that "Amway" is merely a tradename must be taken seriously.

22. In a World Where So Many Are Poor and Hungry, It Bothers Me to Hear People Talk About Yachts and Diamond Rings. Is It Fair to Describe Amway as Encouraging Materialism?

Amway is a business, and a business cannot survive unless it makes money. Whatever stories you may have heard about the various spin-off results of being an Amway distributor—more friends, better self-esteem, and the like—may well be true, but Amway is first, last, and always a business. Its primary purpose is not political, religious, or altruistic; its purpose is to put dollars into people's pockets to enable them to buy material things.

Amway goes beyond that most basic definition of a business, however, and encourages its distributors to aspire to a higher standard of living. If you live in a small house and want to live in a larger house, Amway says, go ahead and admit to that desire, make it a goal to get the new house, and go to work for it. And if you already live in a large house, then it's okay to want a boat, or a Mercedes, or a summer home on the lake. The Amway attitude is that wanting expensive material things should be an acceptable desire for people so long as they are willing to work hard and honestly to acquire them.

To want more—more money, comforts, and things—and to express openly that hunger, is a common element in the Amway attitude: If you work hard to get it, if you are not taking it away from someone else, what's wrong with wanting more?

The thing that makes Amway so susceptible to criticism about materialism is that the "more" which Amway people want, and often get, can be truly spectacular. There is so much income potential in a well-developed Amway distributorship that "Diamonds" and "Crowns" sometimes earn the kind of money that can put a very expensive lifestyle within their reach. And that is usually when the criticism begins.

When the Chevy's become Cadillacs, and the rabbit coats become full-length mink, and the weekends at the beach become summers in Europe, critical Amway-watchers begin dusting off their arguments about how bad it is to have it so good.

The average American seems to have almost a love-hate relationship with money. Though our society has always applauded initiative and hard work, we tend to become uneasy if someone with initiative works hard and as a result becomes wealthy. Suddenly we wonder if that person's wealth is somehow a betrayal of all the people who have so much less.

Loudon Wainwright, in a recent bit of social commentary in *Life* magazine, admits to this sort of ambivalence about money: "The subject of money arouses strong feelings in me: guilt (because I don't think I deserve it), fear (because I might lose it), and ignorance (because I can't manage it). Also envy (because I want more) and shame (because I know it). In short, I bring about as little objectivity to the subject as the next man. Alert to signs of avarice in myself, I'm not slow to spot them in others. I despise the lackey in me who fawns on wealth and power, possibly because I know I might happily submit to such fawning myself. When H. Ross Perot walks by, I try—without much success—to look right through him."

Amway has an excellent record of social responsibility— major gifts to churchs, hospitals, schools, and the arts, and nationwide efforts in such charities as the Easter Seals campaign, for example—and points out that many of its distributors are also heavy contributors to all manner of causes. Still, Amway people must frequently explain their view that being a man or woman of means should not be a thing for which one apologizes.

Rich DeVos probably says it best: "Some seem to believe that if the rich have less the poor will have more. That is not the case. If those who have material wealth have less, then everyone has less. If you want the caboose to catch up with the locomotive, you don't do it by stopping the train."

Another point should be made before rushing to convict Amway on a "materialism" charge. However much one hears of yachts and diamond rings, most of those Amway bonus dollars are spent in less exotic ways. The majority of Amway distributors have not yet reached that rarefied level and are happy to cash their Amway checks to buy shoes for the kids, pay the extra bills that always appear at the end of the month, and finance an occasional night out on the town. People do get rich in Amway, but for every one who does so, there are many more who simply get comfortable. And there is a lot to be said for that.

23. Is It True That a Person Can Continue Making Money From an Amway Business Even After He or She Stops Working?

The prospect of developing this type of "walkaway income" is probably the single biggest attraction of businesses like Amway. Yes, it is possible, after building a solid Amway business, to have a li'l ol' money-making machine that keeps pumping out income after the distributor no longer works at it very hard personally.

Sprawling on a remote beach while royalty checks pour into one's mailbox is a tantalizing prospect. The key to it is the phrase "*after* building a solid Amway business." That is a critical prerequisite, and one which people—inside and outside Amway—occasionally overlook. Building such a business is a major challenge; anyone who believes it will happen easily also believes in the Tooth Fairy and Jolly Old Saint Nicholas.

What is extraordinary is that such a thing is possible at all, and it clearly is possible within the Amway structure. The Amway plan includes various payoffs which are similar to the royalty payments received by the author of a book, or recording artist, or the owner of an oil well. One writes a book and is paid immediately for the work done; but if the book is still selling years later, and therefore making a profit for its publisher, then a small percentage of that profit is in turn paid to the author, long after the original work has been done.

Likewise for a bestselling record, or a movie, or a coal mine or natural gas well. For as many years as that item makes money for anyone at all, the person who produced it in the first place is entitled to a piece of the profits. Amway Corporation rewards every individual distributorship on that basis. If you build an Amway business, as long as that business is producing income for the corporation and you meet certain standards, you share in that income. It is this feature of the Amway plan which has created many of those almost-unbelievable success stories which make up the Amway folklore.

24. Aren't Almost All Amway Distributors Right-Wing Conservative Types?

Amway tends to attract people with fairly conservative social and political views. It has a history of supporting traditional values, and its co-founders are personally involved in a variety of conservative political activities.

But it is inaccurate to describe the distributor force as being "a bunch of right-wingers." Amway distributors are drawn more or less representatively from the population as a whole, and reflect the pluralism of the American people itself. That heterogeneous mix is increasing in Amway. The distributor force fifteen years ago was undoubtedly more stereotypically WASP-ish than it is today. One of the most dramatic trends in Amway in the 1980s has been the increasing number of black, Hispanic, Jewish, and Asian-American distributors.

The first breakthrough into the ranks of Amway "diamonds" by a black distributorship was achieved by George and Ruth Halsey, an eloquent husband-wife team from

Greensboro, North Carolina, who broke the color barrier in 1978. Since then, dozens of black distributors have reached that level, and the Halseys have themselves gone on to become Triple Diamonds. Today, there are tens of thousands of black and other minority Amway distributors, and outside observers who come to Amway meetings expecting to see a lily-white crowd are surprised to find such ethnic diversity.

Politically, too, Amway has become less monolithic. Though a political preference poll would undoubtedly show the distributor force to be predominantly Republican, there are signs of a healthy Democratic presence growing in Amway ranks. When Governor Reuben Askew, a Florida Democrat, made a brief run for his party's presidential nomination in 1984, Amway distributors were his principal campaign workers. The New York *Times* referred to Amway distributors as "the backbone of the Askew organization" in the Iowa Democratic caucuses. The Atlanta *Journal*, in an analysis of Askew's Iowa chances, said that a "network of Amway distributors" constituted his major source of support.

This is not to suggest that Tip O'Neill is likely to be voted Amway's Man of the Year anytime soon. Nothing quite so drastic as that. Gay rights and unilateral disarmament are still not popular causes at an Amway rally. But it does suggest that the "right-wing fanatic" label does not fit the Amway distributor force very well, and is becoming increasingly less applicable.

Van Andel, who like his partner is personally committed to the traditional conservative agenda of Republicans like Presidents Ford and Reagan, nevertheless applauds the development of sociopolitical diversity in the Amway ranks. "We believe there should be room in Amway for people of every political view," he has said. "This company reflects America, and America is a land of rich pluralism, a land where people respect one another's right to political differences. I would like to think Amway is a part of that tradition, and we're doing whatever we can to see that it is."

25. I've Heard Amway Is Anti-Union. True or Untrue?

Amway is not anti-union, and could hardly afford to be, since many of its distributors are members of various labor unions in their full-time jobs. The corporation is emphatically *non*-union, however, and corporate officials insist that the distinction is a real one. Manufacturing and other corporate functions are operated on an open-shop basis.

26. Is It True That if I Get Into Amway I Must Start by Working for Another Distributor?

Not exactly. The only way to become an Amway distributor is to be "sponsored" by an existing distributor. There are no exceptions to this rule. If you picked up the phone, called Amway corporate headquarters, and asked to become a distributor, you would be given a list of distributors in your local area and told to get in touch with one of them. The corporation itself will not bring you into the distributor force—only another distributor can.

But you won't be working *for* that distributor. When she sponsors you, she makes a promise to provide you with products and the necessary training to get started. She is not in any sense your boss or your employer. The Amway plan gives her a financial interest in your success as a new distributor, however, so that she has a strong incentive to give you all the support possible. The distributor who sponsors you gets nothing for merely signing you up; the payoff for her is based not on recruiting you, but on your success *after* you sign up.

The relationship between Amway distributors and the people who sponsor them varies widely from case to case. In some instances, new distributors have literally never seen their sponsors again after signing up, and have gone on independently to build big businesses. In other cases, the new distributor and his or her sponsor become close friends and work together as virtual partners for many years. Amway Corporation leaves that relationship entirely up to the distributors themselves.

27. What Guarantee Is There That a New Amway Distributor Will Make a Profit?

There is none. Amway operates strictly on the principle of paying you for what you produce, no more and no less. That means that some people sign up as Amway distributors and never make a dime. There are several ways of making money in Amway, however, and some of them are fairly simple. The distributor who engages in the basic steps of the business-building plan is likely to begin earning a small profit almost immediately, with the larger payoffs coming in later stages. But there is no guaranteed salary or income for the beginning distributor.

28. How Long Must Distributors Be in the Amway Business Before They Can Sign Up New Distributors to Work for Them?

A new distributor can sponsor other distributors into the business immediately. There is no waiting period. The reasoning behind this policy, according to Amway, is that individuals who are starting a business should be allowed to share the experience with friends from the very beginning. An individual can literally become an Amway distributor one day and bring a new person into the business the next day.

This is not to say, however, that the new distributor will be working "for" the sponsor. In Amway, no one works "for" anyone else. (More about that in question 26.)

29. I've Always Thought of Amway as a Door-to-Door Business, but a Friend of Mine Who Is in It Insists It Isn't Door-to-Door. Who Is Right?

Amway doesn't like the phrase "door-to-door," regards it as having undesirable connotations, and insists that it is inaccurate when applied to its distributors.

Amway is a "direct-sales" company, which means that its products are sold by individuals rather than in stores or other retail outlets. But Amway distributors are discouraged from random peddling of their products to strangers; instead, they rely on what they call "person-to-person" sales, making customers of friends, family members, people they already know.

In Amway's earliest days as a new company, some distributors did sell products on a door-to-door basis. Today's pattern of merchandising, a more professional and efficient "person-to-person" approach, has gradually evolved, and much of the general public is simply unaware of that change. Hence the frequent description of Amway as a door-to-door company. Old images die hard.

30. I Heard a Rumor That Michael Jackson Is an Amway Distributor. If That Is True, Why Would a Celebrity Like Him Want to Sell Amway?

Michael Jackson is not an Amway distributor. That the rumor should circulate, however, is not unusual; over the years dozens of celebrities from Johnny Carson to Sammy Davis Jr. to President Ronald Reagan have been reported to be Amway distributors, in most cases erroneously. The corporate public relations office periodically is called upon by the media to shoot down such rumors.

Amway Corporation's posture toward celebrity involvement has been to pay little attention to it when it does occur.

Such public figures as Pat Boone, civil rights activist James Meredith, and Connecticut Senator Lowell Weicker, along with many other celebrities, have been Amway distributors in the past without drawing attention from Amway itself. "Our policy," says a corporate official, "is not to make public notice of who our distributors are. That is just as true when the individual happens to be a famous person. It's just not a big deal to us."

31. How Is It Possible for People to Make Fifty Thousand Dollars a Year Working Three to Four Hours a Week in Their Spare Time? It Just Doesn't Make Sense to Me.

It shouldn't. For a deal that good, you need a mask and a gun. Fifty thousand dollars a year for three-to-four hours' work a week is an unreasonable expectation, and anyone who promises it for Amway or any other business will probably also offer you swampland in Florida if you indicate an interest in real estate.

The fifty thousand a year is not the unreasonable part. Many people build Amway businesses which produce that much income and more. But they invariably have done so with a major commitment of time and effort.

At the same time, there are many Amway distributors who work at it only three-to-four hours a week—or even less. But they earn modest amounts, and usually have come into the business in hopes of making a little extra money on the side, rather than as a major career move.

So you can make big money in Amway or you can work at it very casually. But you can't do both, at least not in the early stages of building a distributorship.

32. How Much Money Must a New Amway Distributor Tie Up in Product Inventory to Get Started?

Literally, none. Designed as it is to be a business within the reach of people without up-front capital to invest, the

Amway plan makes it possible for a distributor to get started with literally zero dollars tied up in product inventory.

The way the system works, a new distributor takes products from the inventory of his or her "direct distributor" and sells it to the retail customer without the necessity of stocking it personally. That system makes it possible for an individual to begin without a major front-end investment.

33. I Had a Friend Who Got Into Amway and Became Totally Obsessed With It. He Breathed It, Ate It for Breakfast, Lunch, and Dinner. Is That What It Takes to Make It Work?

Of course not. The obsessive plunge into Amway you describe is not necessary for success, but the symptoms do sound familiar: this type of preoccupation with a new activity frequently occurs when individuals lock on to projects which fully engage their abilities, their emotions, and their energy. It sometimes happens with a graduate student in an academic program which is genuinely enjoyable. Or with a good athlete who takes up a new sport, such as skiing, and seems unable to even think about anything else.

Such total involvement is frequently seen with new Amway distributors, especially those who are doing well. The challenge of building an Amway business calls upon such a wide range of the person's abilities and emotions that it can be an exhilarating experience for many people, and they often plunge into it with an unusual level of enthusiasm.

The fear that such a total immersion in the Amway experience leaves people permanently out of synch with the non-Amway world seems to be unfounded, however.

34. I Heard Amway Recently Laid Off Hundreds of Employees at Its Plant in Michigan. Isn't That a Bad Sign?

Amway did lay off several hundred of its seven thousand employees in early 1984. It was the first time in the company's history for such a workforce reduction, and newspapers around the country carried a wire-service story describing the layoffs.

What the newspapers have not reported is that within a year all the laid-off production workers had been quietly re-hired, and as of early 1985 are back on the job.

35. Amway Seems to Be Built Around Van Andel and DeVos. What Happens When They Aren't There to Run It Anymore?

This could be a problem, but the owners themselves insist it is one they have anticipated and made contingency plans to cover.

In the early years of Amway's growth, the company had the style and personality of a large family. Most of the leading distributors knew one another and were on a first-name basis with DeVos and Van Andel. Though the two founders still actively operate the company and make major decisions, the daily management is increasingly done by their executive staff.

According to *Venture* magazine, Amway is the third-largest company in America which is still owned and managed by its original founders. When they no longer lead the company on a daily basis, second-generation DeVoses and Van Andels are likely to move into their positions. But that too is only speculation. For now the co-founders are healthy, active, and relatively young. They both demonstrate great appetites for leading the company into its next period of growth, and there is little reason to believe they will not be around for many years. In the event of some personal catastrophe that might take either of them off the scene, they declare that a contingency plan is in place to keep Amway moving ahead without interruption.

36. Why Does Amway Seem to Get Such Bad Coverage in the Press?

Whenever a new phenomenon appears on the national landscape, whether a political candidate, a medical breakthrough, or something like Amway, the media attention given to it follows a predictable cyclic pattern.

First there is the "discovery stage," when the idea is new and interesting, and the press rushes to describe it to the public in an uncritical and usually admiring way. After a wave of that kind of attention, the press grows tired of repeating the same positive things, and the "downside stage" is reached. In this stage, coverage seems to tilt toward the negative aspects of the phenomenon. Reporters approach their stories with an eye to exposing feet of clay, competing with one another to demythologize this thing which has heretofore sounded too good to be true. Finally, this negative slant grows stale, just as the positive did, and a third stage, the "balanced stage," is reached, in which the matter at hand is no longer new and exciting, and journalistic attention becomes evenhanded and routine.

Media-watchers see this pattern repeated countless times, with all sorts of subjects, sometimes cycling over a period of a few weeks, sometimes over a period of several years. The Gary Hart political phenomenon in the winter of 1984 is a good example. His candidacy became a national news story literally overnight, when he upset his Democratic opponents in the New Hampshire presidential primary. For the next few weeks he was the fair-haired boy of the media: how fresh, how charismatic, how like the Kennedys, how covered with grace and promise was this Gary Hart! Then, having exhausted all those angles, the next set of stories began: the name-change stories, the bad-marriage stories, the stories that declared the Hart candidacy to be a triumph of style over substance. Finally, the needle swung back toward the middle, and Gary Hart at last began to get balanced coverage.

Consider the media attention to a phenomenon as trivial as break dancing. First, how cute it is. Next, the but-on-the-other-hand stories about how it may *look* cute, but it gives little boys stress fractures and sprained wrists. Then, finally, the ho-hum stage. Or consider as serious a subject as the implantation of a mechanical heart into a human patient: first, we hear how daring, how brilliant, how dedicated the surgeons and brave the patient. Then the emphasis swings to the downside: questions about the costliness of the procedure, the moral implications of human experimentation, the concerns about runaway technology and who should choose the recipients of such treatment. Until finally a stage of less value-ridden reporting is reached.

Amway is experiencing this same cycle of media attention. Amway is not just another corporation; the media are certainly aware of that, and approach it not just as a business, but as a "socioreligious phenomenon of some sort," as one magazine described it. The press has always seen Amway as a movement with social and political implications far beyond those of other companies its size.

For the first dozen years or so, from 1959 until the early or mid-1970s, Amway was too small to be much noticed. As it reached the quarter-billion mark in sales, and its distributor force began to number in the hundreds of thousands, the press "discovered" Amway, and for a few years it enjoyed very favorable media attention. It was portrayed as a fresh, unconventional way of doing business, an example of middle-American innovation, of heartland values asserting themselves—a Norman Rockwell painting come to life.

That period of uncritical attention could not be expected to continue, and it didn't. As the 1970s slid over into the eighties, stage two was reached, and Amway is just now, in 1985, emerging from it. Weary of hearing how it is the greatest thing since seedless watermelon, the press set out to find the downside of the Amway phenomenon, and the result has been a wave of national and local coverage that has emphasized the flaws, the problems, and the "other side" of the story. That phase appears to be ending, and Amway, having survived its rite of passage into the ranks of major American corporations, is already beginning to get more positive, balanced treatment in the press.

It may have seemed to Amway people, during the period of negative press, that the media pursued the dark side of their story with greater enthusiasm than they reported the positive side. This is probably true, not because of some specific antagonism toward Amway, but because it is the nature of the press—and the general public as well—to find bad news more interesting than good. John Steinbeck once observed: "We value virtue, but do not discuss it. The honest bookkeeper, the faithful wife, the earnest scholar get little of our attention compared to the embezzler, the tramp, and the cheat."

That natural bias, always a sizable one, was reinforced by the social dynamics of the Watergate and Vietnam episodes during the 1970s, in which the "establishment" almost always turned out to wear the black hat and the press the white hat. It was not those reporters who wrote heartwarming stories from the heartland who became national heroes, but those who exposed deceit and chicanery in high places. In the post-Watergate era, it seemed, the only big news was bad news, and it was in this period that Amway came of age.

There is another factor which has contributed to Amway's public-image problems, and that is the very nature of the business operation itself. Amway is not a single, tightly controlled corporate monolith, like Bethlehem Steel or Lockheed, with x number of employees who make products sold by a salaried marketing department to y number of customers. Amway is one million people operating mostly from their homes, all owning their own private distributorships, each of them representing—or misrepresenting—the Amway experience to some neighborhood, community, or circle of friends. From a public-relations standpoint, that is a high-risk way of doing business.

Amway Corporation is so totally committed to the princi-

ple of open admission to its distributor force that it chooses to
live with the public-relations liabilities rather than abandon
that policy. Amway could undoubtedly reduce its vulnera-
bility in the press by screening applicants for distributorships, making admission to its ranks more selective. Or it
could also control potential public-relations problems by
imposing tighter control on the distributor force.

But Amway officials protest that either course would take
it away from one of its most basic traditional values—that of
a free, open opportunity to own and operate one's business
for oneself. They point out that part of Amway's magic is
that it does not impose such restrictions on joining. "Too
many business opportunities already are closed to the man
or woman with no capital or specialized training," says Van
Andel. "It is in that sense that the American dream has become more and more limited. At Amway we are committed
to keeping the door of opportunity open to Everyman, not
just to those who have financial or personal resources available to them. Of course we could avoid some problems by
becoming more exclusive, but where would that leave those
whom we exclude? In order to offer a truly open opportunity, we're willing to take a few risks."

37. What Kind of People Usually Turn Out to Be Successful in an Amway Distributorship?

There is no good answer to that question. When the demo-
graphics are sifted and sorted, no reliable pattern emerges.

Naturally, the characteristics that contribute to success in
other areas are helpful in Amway, so those people with
records of success in education, other business ventures, or
professional careers are logically good bets for success in
Amway as well. But predicting a successful distributorship
on that basis alone doesn't work very well in practice, since
there is a high percentage of big, lucrative Amway businesses
being built by men and women whose previous track records
include few successes.

The pattern is so common in Amway that it has become a cliché: an individual with no money, no college training, no exceptional personality comes into the business and scores big. Those examples seem to defy any attempt at demographic classification, and there are so many legitimate rags-to-riches stories in Amway that one can hardly regard them as exceptions to the rule.

On the other hand, the more recent period of Amway growth—especially in the last ten years—has included a very high percentage of professional men and women who bring all their upper-middle-class resources to the process. In the early years of Amway's history, there was a notion that its appeal was limited to the blue-collar and wage-earning public. Many people, inside and outside Amway, thought of it as actually working better among people with fewer career options, and expected the handful of professionals who came into the business to have a tough time selling the concept to their peers. That has proved not to be true; obviously it works just as well in the upscale part of town as anywhere else.

Another popular idea is that Amway is particularly suitable for individuals who are highly articulate, persuasive types. Although the business includes its share of high-octane talkers, the majority of successful distributors do not fit this stereotype at all. They are not likely to be any more skilled speakers than the general population, at least not when they initially come into the business. They may learn to be better speakers as they build their businesses, but the standard joke among distributors goes like this: "When I got into this business I was so timid I couldn't even lead in silent prayer!"

A common notion about Amway is that when a person becomes a distributor, he or she immediately begins standing up before a roomful of people to smooth-talk and razzle-dazzle them into doing something they don't want to do. If that were true, few people would possess the persuasive skills to do the job. Actually, the business does not operate that way at all. In the early stages of a new distributorship, someone else is typically "showing the plan" and doing whatever persuading is necessary. An individual can build a business to considerable size before ever having to deal with the problem of stage fright.

Many outsiders who meet big-time Amway leaders for the first time are surprised that they do not fit the high-pressure, go-go stereotype. They find instead that most high-achieving Amway distributors who have built large businesses look and sound about like themselves—not glib and gifted Superman or Supergirl types who knock people's socks off just by walking into a room. They are more likely to be "ordinary" people who have created extraordinary success by working very hard.

Other than that, it is difficult to identify a particular profile which leads to fame and fortune in Amway. The Diamond roll call includes all kinds of occupations, backgrounds, ethnic groups, ages, and personality types.

38. Amway's Sales Volume Decreased Last Year. Does That Mean the Bubble Is About to Burst?

Amway did have a decrease in sales volume in 1983, for the first time in its history. (This was true in North America only; volume in international markets continue to rise.) The company's corporate revenues dipped from $1.4 billion in 1982 to $1.1 billion in 1983, and stayed at that level in 1984.

Analysts of the direct-sales industry feel that this reduced volume is attributable to pressures in the general marketplace rather than any problems specific to Amway itself. Every established direct-sales company experienced a similar downward squiggle in its sales graph during these two years, industry experts point out. Avon, Mary Kay Cosmetics, Tupperware, and Shaklee all experienced problems at least as bad as Amway's. Mary Kay, for example, suffered through a 65 percent drop in its stock value during 1983, and Tupperware saw profits "tumble sharply," according to the Chicago *Tribune*.

Wall Street analyst Emma Hill of Wertheim and Company, a New York investment firm, blames the improvement in the economy for the troubles in the direct-sales industry, along with a proliferation of direct-sales companies, from 250 of them in 1980 to over 400 by 1984.

An analyst with the Morgan Stanley firm concurs with that view. In an interview in *Working Mother* magazine, direct-sales expert Brenda Landry stated: "In a sentence, the pool of part-time workers in the U.S. probably shrank somewhat in 1983 at a time when the number of part-time jobs available was rising."

Most industry observers agree that the dip in sales experienced by Amway, along with other direct-sales firms, is a natural response to the cyclic nature of the national economy, and expect the charts to show upward movement again. Amway officials take the view that no company, however exceptional, can go indefinitely without some sort of ebb and flow. Not even Amway, they say, can expect to avoid ever having a down year. After twenty-three consecutive years of growth, a lull in the company's climb was inevitable, they say, and does not indicate any long-term weakness in the appeal of Amway to the consumer or the prospective distributor.

There are signs that Amway may come out of this period of direct-sales woes with a more streamlined, efficient company. In the past year DeVos and Van Andel have authorized a wall-to-wall restructuring of the corporate staff, and begun an aggressive program of developing new products. Both men seem to be responding to the challenges of the mid-1980s with a fresh burst of the competitive zeal that built Amway in the first place.

"We didn't build this thing around crying about what happened last night or last year," DeVos says. "We've made something from nothing. And we're going to continue to make it work."

· 10 ·

FACES IN THE CROWD

The portrait of Amway which the public usually sees is a group portrait, a crowd shot. It is possible to give so much attention to defining the "average" or "typical" Amway distributor that one overlooks the individual faces in the crowd. A roster of Amway distributors may have more interesting characters per capita than any other group of businesspeople around.

It is the successful, high-profile Amway winners who attract the attention of the public, those unusual individuals who have dug into the Amway treasure trove and come out with a full share of its goodies. Amway tends to attract—and to reward—men and women with extraordinary amounts of energy, ambition, and vision of their own futures, and that kind of person stands out in any crowd.

Here is a small and more or less random collection of several Amway distributors who, if they lived in your community, would undoubtedly attract your neighbors' attention. These are the kind of Amway people Amway-watchers like to watch:

MR. AND MRS. AMERICA

If you wished to show your mother how fine, how wholesome, how totally admirable is Amway, you could hardly do better than to take Paul and Debbie Miller home for Sunday dinner. They are freshly scrubbed, clean-cut, All-American models of the entire set of positive values which Amway represents.

The Millers are in their early thirties, and live in the Raleigh, North Carolina, area. Their life sounds like something from a storybook. He was a college football star at the University of North Carolina, quick and smart and the kind who says "sir" to the coach without being told. He was one of those athletes the girls chase after, but who seem not to notice. And Debbie was every bit his match. She was a majorette at Wake Forest, pretty enough to make the guys in the bleachers wish they had brought their binoculars. They met at a wedding. Violins played. It was perfect.

The way this story usually ends is the football player becomes a balding has-been with a paunch who sells used cars and drinks a lot, and the majorette is dowdy and frustrated by the age of thirty. With the Millers it hasn't turned out that way. He went to law school and became a successful attorney; she kept her smile and her figure; everything they touched turned to gold.

Including an Amway business. They became distributors while Paul was still in law school, and today lead an enormous distributorship which cranks up so much money that he eventually closed his law office to enjoy it on a full-time basis. She raises her family and shares the Amway partnership and looks great. He runs the business and plays a lot of tennis—on his private court, of course—and looks great too.

Want to show your mother the "new Amway"? Take the Millers home for Sunday dinner sometime. It doesn't get any better than that.

O CANADA!

Some individuals reflect and express their geographic regions to an unusual degree—they are virtual symbols of the place that produced them. Jim Janz is that kind of man. A native of western Canada, he lives with his wife, Sharon, in Vancouver, where they have built an Amway business which is one of the biggest in North America.

Janz has a personal style that captures the energy and vitality, the frontier spirit, the irrepressible can-do attitude that marks the Western Canadian temperament. Somebody should put him on a poster as a Royal Canadian Mounted Policeman. He is a big man; when he gets excited he doesn't talk, he booms; when he laughs the room shakes; and when he moves into action, things get done.

Jim and Sharon grew up in Alberta in a conservative religious environment, and he was teaching school in Calgary when they came into Amway twenty years ago. Much has changed in those decades—the penniless schoolteacher has become an important community leader with wealth and influence he never expected or even sought. But the basic things in the Janz life have not changed: they are still deeply involved in Christian causes; they still regard their home and spiritual commitments as their highest priorities; and Sharon still has a smile that can melt a country boy's heart at forty paces. What has changed is that now, compared to 1964, they have more time and money to give to the causes they support—and, as a full partner in the Janz business empire, Sharon has more to smile about.

THE PROFESSIONAL WHO LEFT IT BEHIND

Tom Payne is a dentist. Correction: Tom Payne *was* a dentist. When he was a dentist, he was a very good one, with one of the most lucrative practices in the entire region around his small hometown of Guntersville, Alabama. He and his wife,

Carolyn, had hacked it out together in their early days: dental school at the University of Alabama, a hitch in the navy which took them to North Africa, and the struggle to get his practice established.

But Tom was hospitalized one day, and though his illness was not a serious one it started him thinking about the fiscal insecurity of a profession which absolutely depends on the professional being there. That was when the Paynes began looking for a second income. They found it in Amway, and now, almost fifteen years later, Tom has sold his practice and lives royally on his very large Amway income.

The Paynes like Guntersville; their house on the lake is almost perfectly matched to their dream of what an ideal home should be, and they see no reason to leave now that they have more time to enjoy it. They also own a mountain home in Big Canoe, Georgia, and a ski condo in Steamboat Springs, Colorado. Their sons attend Baylor School, a very exclusive, very expensive prep school in Chattanooga. They seem not to miss dentistry—the Amway business, they say, has given them all the rewards dentistry offered, with more security and fewer hassles.

JUST ONE BIG HAPPY FAMILY

Amway people frequently speak of their organizations as being "like one big happy family." When it is the Delisles, of the San Jose area of northern California, who say it, the cliché can be taken quite literally.

Frank and Rita Delisle moved to the Bay Area in 1962. Frank had been a printer in Massachusetts, moved to California in search of the promised land, and found it not in the usual places but in the Amway business. After a few months in Amway, he quit his job as a printer, and has earned his living from Amway ever since. The elder Delisles are now Crowns, making far more money than the highest-paying job at the company where he worked before.

The unusual thing about the Delisle story is that they had

two sons, Frank Jr. and Dennis, who were young teenagers when their parents entered Amway. Both sons were so convinced of the potential of the Amway business that they never took up any other career. Both have built separate distributorships, along with their wives, to the level of six-figure incomes, and have never worked for anyone or anything else.

THE DREAM BUILDER

When you hear people talk of those rare, charismatic individuals, those natural leaders, those men whom other men and women seem willing to follow anywhere—they are talking about men like Dexter Yager. He is perhaps the epitome of the big-time Amway distributor, with all the trappings of enormous success: wealth, thousands of loyal followers, and influence with the shakers and movers of politics, entertainment, and religion. It is said that the list of senators and governors who answer Yager's telephone calls is a very long one. He is a man to reckon with.

He got that way through building an Amway business. Growing up in a small town in upstate New York, no one would have predicted that Yager would ever become a major force in anything worthwhile. He and his wife, Birdie, eked out a living from his job with a beer distributor. They lived in a small house and drove an old, rusted-out car. He had no specialized skills, little education, and seemed stuck in the same rut that had claimed most of his friends.

But when Amway crossed his path, it unlocked the extraordinary talents which have made him one of Amway's biggest legends. The nature of Yager's leadership is difficult to define. Not a physically imposing person, not a particularly gifted speaker in the conventional sense, he nonetheless seems able to bring alive the dreams and ambitions which lie dormant in other people. Yager makes people believe in themselves.

Now living in Charlotte, North Carolina, the Yagers have been the focus of much media attention. Their Amway success and its accompanying lifestyle has been described in newspaper and magazine articles, on national television, and undoubtedly in a million living-room conversations. It is a classic rags-to-riches Amway story, a dramatic example of how far from one's beginnings one can travel in this kind of business.

THE ODD COUPLE

Two Amway leaders who often conduct meetings as partners in Haverhill, Massachusetts, offer a sharp example of the kind of contrasts one finds among successful Amway people. One is a short, white, former service-station operator; the other is a black psychologist with a Ph.D. They have almost nothing in common except their business, but make perfect partners in Amway.

OUT OF THE BASEMENT

A leading Amway official recently described the new direction of the company as "coming out of the basement and headed for Main Street." He was referring to the growing number of career-oriented couples who are bringing to Amway a style of professionalism and strategic marketing which it has not known in earlier years.

The prototype of this new breed of young Amway professionals is Jim and Nancy Dornan, an attractive young Southern California couple who are among the company's top distributors. Jim was an engineer, a Purdue graduate, and Nancy a speech therapist when they entered Amway in the early 1970s. He quit his job at Douglas Aircraft within a year of starting their distributorship, and since then has pursued his Amway career with all the seriousness of any upward-mobile professional.

"This is a business, and we treat it like one," he says. "This is not a funny little soap thing that we do on the side for some extra money. It's a challenging, rewarding management and marketing career—plenty complex enough to keep someone interested." The success of the Dornans' approach is evident: they are Crown distributors and travel across the country many times each year to tell other distributors how they do it. "I didn't get into Amway to sleep until noon," says Dornan. "We try to bring to our business the same degree of professionalism that successful people in other careers bring to their work." For the Dornans, at least, it obviously pays off.

LIVING WELL IS THE BEST REVENGE

Tim and Sherry Bryan were a hardworking young couple, with three small children, in Portland, Maine. He was a high-school teacher; she was a legal secretary; both were frustrated because they seemed never to get ahead, always feeling the pressure of not having enough money.

When they decided to join Amway, nobody encouraged them. Many of Sherry's colleagues at the office told her she was nuts for trying. Friends told them they could never do it. They invited twenty-three couples to their first meeting, and no one showed up. Tim remembers being so scared before he showed the plan that some nights he would become literally nauseated on the way to the meetings, and would stop the car alongside the road until the sickness passed.

But they persisted, and their business took hold. Today they are a prosperous family living in a fashion that seemed a fantasy a few years ago. "My first dream was to move out of our little apartment into a double-wide mobile home," Sherry remembers, "and we eventually moved into a house next door to the attorney who was my boss before Amway."

What is the biggest payoff to Tim and Sherry? Maybe this one: "The girls in the office gave me a hard time about leaving my kids at night to build our Amway business. That hurt. But five years later they are still working—and they're mothers too—and I'm home with my kids every day. I had twins and started them in nursery school at two-and-a-half-years old. I missed a lot of their growing up. Now with my little one, I'm there for all the first steps, everything. That's what Amway has given Tim and me."

THE ODD COUPLE, PART II

Two distributors who work together in California and Utah could hardly have less similar occupations. One is a high-school dropout who was working as a garbage collector. He sponsored a medical doctor whose specialty was psychiatry. Both built successful direct distributorships. In this case, it was the garbage collector who provided the advice and leadership for the psychiatrist. Was he intimidated by having a psychiatrist in his group? "No," he explains, "I used him as an example to all my friends. I told them that if a shrink could do this business, a sanitation worker should have no problem with it at all!"

FROM MR. STUTTER TO MR. SMOOTH

Can Amway really change a person's life? Financially, of course, but can it change a person's life in other ways as well?

Dan Williams will tell you it can. He is one of Amway's most polished platform speakers, featuring streams of one-liners that would make Bob Hope envious. When Amway people talk about the best public speakers they have heard, the name Dan Williams always comes up.

But it was not always that way. To the contrary, in Dan's pre-Amway days, when he and his wife, Bunny, lived on an engineer's salary in Baton Rouge, Louisiana, he stuttered so badly he could hardly be understood. He tried every possible cure: drugs, psychotherapy, hypnosis, speech clinics. Nothing helped.

When he became an Amway distributor, it was for the typical reason—to make more money. But as his business grew, so did his self-confidence, and his preoccupation with his speech problem diminished correspondingly. Within several months, the Williamses had not only a growing Amway business, but the totally unexpected bonus of a cure for Dan's stuttering problem.

That was more than a dozen years ago. Today Dan and Bunny Williams live in a palatial mansion in Santa Barbara, California. They are admired as top Amway leaders by a network of tens of thousands of distributors in their extended organization. And they have the sense of style and poise that fits their upscale image. The people in Dan's audiences these days would never guess that he has ever been anything but Mr. Smooth. But he and Bunny know, more than most, that in Amway lots of things can change, and that means more than money.

THE SKI-LIFT CONNECTION

Where do Amway distributors find people to sponsor?

For a pair of Diamond distributors, the matchup occurred literally on a ski lift. Chuck and Jean Strehli are among the top leaders in the Amway business. A law student at the University of Texas when he came into Amway, Chuck enjoyed the business so much that he never practiced law, going full-time in Amway immediately upon receiving his degree.

When he and Jean were skiing on a vacation a few years ago, he found himself riding a lift with a young engineer. By the time they reached the top of the mountain, Chuck had learned that his fellow passenger was also a Texan, and the two couples got together for dinner later that week. They stayed in touch with Don and Gretchen Seagren, and soon sponsored them into Amway. The Seagrens went on to become Diamonds themselves—the Strehlis are Crowns—and are now full-time Amway professionals. The four have since skied together in the Alps.

In Amway, they call this sort of thing "work." It's a tough life.

BUTTON-DOWN COLLARS AND GRAY-FLANNEL SUITS

In case you've been convinced that very successful Amway distributors are all rambunctious, supercharged types who base their success on flamboyance and adrenaline, take a long look at Brian Hays, who with his wife, Marg, is probably the leading Amway figure in the Chicago area.

Brian Hays looks the part of the quintessential corporation man: calm, smiling, neatly groomed, ever-so-polite, with an air of quiet competence. He has a boyish face and a computer for a brain. Companies like IBM should keep Brian Hays in a frozen-food locker and clone him for all their junior executives. And Marg holds up her end of the image: she is Junior League all the way, beautifully tailored, unfailingly charming. She is so youthful looking, she and her daughter might turn up in one of those "which one is the mother?" commercials on TV someday.

Brian and Marg came to Amway from the corporate backgrounds which their styles suggest. He was a Motorola executive who stayed with his corporation long after he could have afforded to leave. He enjoyed the life of a corporate exec, but eventually tired of it. He knew he didn't want to punch an executive timeclock, even a gold-plated one, for the rest of his life. So, after saving his Motorola paychecks for several months, just to make sure he wouldn't miss them, he left the company for a full-time Amway career.

The actress Elizabeth Ashley once explained it this way: "You get tired of tap-dancing after a while, even if you enjoy it." Brian Hays would certainly agree.

THERE GOES ANOTHER STEREOTYPE

When it comes to smashing Amway stereotypes, Stuart Menn is a one-man wrecking crew. Ever have someone try to tell you that all the big hitters in Amway are (1) blue-collar, (2) Protestant, (3) small-town (4) married men (5) from the

Midwest? Stuart Menn is one of the most successful Amway Diamonds in the country, and he is none of the above. He is a Jewish medical doctor who is a bachelor from the Bronx now living in San Diego.

THANK GOD I'M A COUNTRY BOY!

Lloyd and Donna Claypool were country kids, born and raised. They grew up as childhood friends in a tiny farming community in southern Illinois. Like many hardworking farm kids, they were hungry for bigger and better things than they had as children, but neither of them wanted to leave their familiar home territory to acquire them.

From the earliest days of their marriage, the Claypools worked together to try to bring a slice of the good life to their part of rural Illinois. Lloyd estimates that during certain seasons it was not uncommon for him to work eighteen hours a day. He and his brother operated a body shop and a twenty-four-hour wrecker service, as well as an auto parts store. That was an eight-to-five job, nonstop, and when he left the shop Lloyd's day was only half over. He was also farming one thousand acres of corn and tending one thousand head of hogs. He went from the shop to the farm, where he worked until two A.M.

Even with all that, and with Donna working as well, the Claypools were unable to achieve a financial breakthrough: they were staying even, but no more. In 1970 their prospects turned even worse. A General Motors strike stopped the supply of auto parts to their store, the price of hogs nosedived, and a corn blight spread across their crops. That was when they decided, busy as they were, to try Amway.

Amway success did not come easily to the Claypools, but it came. "We didn't set any records," says Lloyd, "but we were always consistent. We were always in there, doing what we could." Apparently that was plenty good enough, for though the Claypools have no story of brilliant, sudden success in Amway, their consistency has placed them in the highest ranks of Amway leaders today.

The Claypools still live in the same small town where they began, but now they live in a "dream home" which is the envy of the entire region, with luxury cars, trips to Europe, and all the other creature comforts that go along with a six-figure income. "We wanted our kids to grow up out in the country," Donna explains. "The grandparents are here and we like it here. Amway gave us the choice to stay and still live like we've always dreamed of living."

LIVING AT THE TOP

William James, one of the first great American psychologists, once said that "human beings really live when they live at the top of their energies."

Few individuals fit that description of "really living" as well as Bill Britt, an Amway leader from Chapel Hill, North Carolina. Britt is the personification of focused, single-minded intensity. He knows what he believes and what he stands for, and he goes after it with the drive and determination of the truly committed. If Amway were the army, Bill Britt would be General George Patton.

If it is easy to imagine Britt leading a platoon of troops into battle, it may be because he has always distinguished himself as a leader. He *was* a military officer, in fact, serving in the Korean War as an army lieutenant. Back home after the war, he entered local government and was a city manager when he and his wife, Peggy, became Amway distributors.

The combination of persistence, leadership, and intense desire which has always been the Britt style was ideally suited to Amway, and he has been a major figure in the business for many years. He has assembled in his organization a team of bright, aggressive young men and women who typify the "new breed" of career Amway distributors. He is on the road constantly, working with them on a one-to-one basis, building the team spirit which pervades his group.

Britt's willingness to pour his energies so totally into his Amway business is rewarded not only by his high income, but also by an unusual level of loyalty and comradeship from the people in his group. To them, he is the best there is. Period. As Tom Wolfe wrote about another leader: "It was as if wherever he landed, the light shone round about him, and that was the place to be."

To Bill Britt, Amway is not just a way of making money. It is a cause, a commitment, a celebration, all rolled into one.

ABOUT THE AUTHOR

CHARLES PAUL CONN is an award-winning free-lance writer whose previous books have appeared on every major bestseller list in America. He holds a Ph.D. in psychology from Emory University, and was a Visiting Scholar at Harvard University in 1981–82. He lives in Cleveland, Tennessee.